Graduate Student and Faculty Spaces and Services

SPEC Kits

Supporting Effective Library Management for Over Thirty Years

Committed to assisting research and academic libraries in the continuous improvement of management systems, ARL has worked since 1970 to gather and disseminate the best practices for library needs. As part of its committment, ARL maintains an active publications program best known for its SPEC Kits. Through the Collaborative Research/Writing Program, librarians work with ARL staff to design SPEC surveys and write publications. Originally established as an information source for ARL member libraries, the SPEC series has grown to serve the needs of the library community worldwide.

What are SPEC Kits?

Published six times per year, SPEC Kits contain the most valuable, up-to-date information on the latest issues of concern to libraries and librarians today. They are the result of a systematic survey of ARL member libraries on a particular topic related to current practice in the field. Each SPEC Kit contains an executive summary of the survey results; survey questions with tallies and selected comments; the best representative documents from survey participants, such as policies, procedures, handbooks, guidelines, Web sites, records, brochures, and statements; and a selected reading list—both print and online sources—containing the most current literature available on the topic for further study.

Subscribe to SPEC Kits

Subscribers tell us that the information contained in SPEC Kits is valuable to a variety of users, both inside and outside the library. SPEC Kit purchasers use the documentation found in SPEC Kits as a point of departure for research and problem solving because they lend immediate authority to proposals and set standards for designing programs or writing procedure statements. SPEC Kits also function as an important reference tool for library administrators, staff, students, and professionals in allied disciplines who may not have access to this kind of information.

SPEC Kits can be ordered directly from the ARL Publications Distribution Center. To order, call **(301) 362-8196**, fax **(301) 206-9789**, e-mail **pubs@arl.org**, or go to **http://www.arl.org/resources/pubs/**.

Information on SPEC Kits and the SPEC survey program can be found at **http://www.arl.org/resources/pubs/spec/index.shtml**. The executive summary for each kit after December 1993 can be accessed free of charge at **http://www.arl.org/resources/pubs/spec/complete.shtml**.

SPEC Kit 308

Graduate Student and Faculty Spaces and Services

November 2008

Vivian Lewis

Associate University Librarian, Organizational Analysis, Planning & Acountability

McMaster University

Cathy Moulder

Director of Library Services, Maps, Data & GIS

McMaster University

ASSOCIATION OF RESEARCH LIBRARIES

Series Editor: Lee Anne George

SPEC Kits are published by the

Association of Research Libraries
21 Dupont Circle, NW, Suite 800
Washington, DC 20036-1118
P (202) 296-2296 F (202) 872-0884
http://www.arl.org/resources/pubs/spec/
pubs@arl.org

ISSN 0160 3582

ISBN 1-59407-807-6
978-1-59407-807-1

Copyright © 2008

♾ The paper used in this publication meets the requirements of ANSI/NISO Z39.48-1992 (R1997) Permanence of
Paper for Publications and Documents in Libraries and Archives.

SPEC Kit 308

Graduate Student and Faculty Spaces and Services
November 2008

SURVEY RESULTS

REPRESENTATIVE DOCUMENTS

Descriptions of Services

Descriptions of Spaces

Position Description

Marketing and Outreach

Partnership Agreement

SELECTED RESOURCES

SURVEY RESULTS

EXECUTIVE SUMMARY

Introduction

Recently, ARL libraries have begun to experiment with an enriched set of spaces and services to meet the complex teaching, learning, and research needs of graduate students and faculty. Some libraries have introduced small sanctuaries (study rooms or lounges) for graduate students and faculty as distinctly separate from undergraduate spaces. Others are providing new suites of services like dissertation support, curriculum design, and learning object design. In some cases, the services are offered in collaboration with other campus units—perhaps the Faculty Development Office, the Learning Technology Office, or Campus Computing. The new services and spaces may be localized in a discrete area (sometimes called a "Research Commons" or "Faculty Commons") or opportunistically distributed across the library system.

The Survey on Graduate Student and Faculty Spaces and Services was conducted to explore the variety of resources and services being delivered to or envisioned for this unique population. The survey was distributed via the Web to the 123 ARL member libraries in March 2008. Sixty-five libraries (six Canadian and 59 American) completed the survey by the deadline of April 28 for a 53% response rate. Of these respondents, 48 institutions (74%) indicated that they provide or plan to provide services or spaces specifically designed for the designated populations. Most are providing or designing spaces/services to meet the needs of both groups, with only seven reporting services/spaces exclusively for graduate students and two locations committed to providing service/space exclusively to faculty. Thirteen of 47 respondents (28%) target discipline-specific graduate students; eight (17%) of these also target a specific group of faculty. In most cases, the targeted groups tend to be in humanities or social sciences.

Developing Graduate Student and/or Faculty Spaces and Services

The ARL libraries responding to the survey reported a wide variety of reasons for introducing services or spaces for these targeted populations. The single biggest motivator was requests from graduate students, reported by 33 institutions (69%), while 25 (52%) reported being influenced by a building renovation or reorganization. Requests from faculty were reported as key factors by 23 respondents (48%), while an equal number reported being persuaded by results of a strategic planning process. Twenty-one libraries reported being influenced by recommendations from library staff.

Respondents employ a wide variety of instruments to gather information about the spaces or services needed—but most reported a reliance on anecdotal feedback. For example, 34 of 43 respondents (79%) reported using informal commentary as part of their decision-making process. Only 20 institutions employed focus groups and only 19 (44%) conducted survey(s) or field observations. Field observations are most frequently used to gather input from library staff, and focus groups and surveys when consulting with faculty or student representatives. Few institutions reported consulting with key campus stakeholders, with only eight libraries (19%) seeking feedback from their student support services offices and six from their faculty development offices. The reliance on current and best practice is more reassuring, with 19 of 36 sites (53%) reporting that their thinking was influenced by literature searches, and an equal number by site visits and expert opinion. Eighteen institutions (50%) were influenced by sessions at conferences, but only seven sites reported being guided by funded research.

Service Location(s) and Descriptions

The physical models vary considerably. Twenty respondents (48%) reported that services are being delivered from pre-existing service points. Eighteen (43%) reported delivering services from a single discrete location, and 14 (33%) deliver services from several new service points dispersed across their campuses.

The majority of facilities are located in renovated space (23 respondents or 77%); the other seven (23%) are located in a combination of new and renovated spaces. No respondents reported placing a service in newly constructed space. The vast majority of respondents (91%) indicated that they provide services to faculty and graduates within the main campus library. A smaller but still sizable percentage (44%) indicated that services are provided within branch libraries; only four respondents said that they offer services in non-library buildings on campus (typically departmental offices or academic buildings).

In some cases, the exclusive nature of the facility or service is designated in its name. Respondents reported a variety of facility names (e.g., the Faculty Support Center, Graduate Student Success Center, Retired Faculty Research Room, Center for Faculty Excellence). Some incorporate the word "Commons" in their name to denote the concept of a gathering place (e.g., Faculty Commons, Research Commons, Scholarly Commons).

Most libraries reported some flexibility in the exclusivity of these services. For example, 26 of 39 respondents (67%) indicated that, although the services had been designed for faculty and/or grads, others could use them under some circumstances. One noted that, although only faculty or grads could reserve the space, others could use it on a drop-in basis. Another noted that the space is typically used for the targeted group but is sometimes opened up for public events. Only 13 institutions (33%) reported that the services were always for the exclusive use of faculty and/or graduate students.

In terms of administrative structure, 37 of the 40 responding institutions report through the library—sometimes to a library director and other times to an AUL, branch head, or other high level administrator. Three institutions also described some accountability to the Provost and one to an academic dean, while one facility also reports through a campus advisory committee. The two facilities that report outside the library are accountable to a CIO or the senior director of the campus computer organization.

Respondents reported a broad range of space offerings, the most common being study seating, lounge seating, and collaborative rooms. Almost all respondents (37 or 90%) provide individual/quiet study seating—six designate this for graduate students exclusively and two for faculty only. Lounge seating is provided at 24 sites (59%)—nine exclusively for graduate students, two exclusively for faculty. Eighteen libraries (44%) provide collaborative rooms, six to graduate students only and three to faculty only. Fewer institutions provide socializing space (12 or 29%), with one restricting this to graduate students and two to faculty exclusively.

Other spaces of interest include recording/videotaping rooms (10 sites or 24%), training spaces (nine or 22%), presentation practice spaces (eight or 20%), performance spaces (seven or 17%), and classrooms (seven or 17%).

The percentage of space allocated to various functions varies considerably. Twenty-six of 29 responding libraries report that space for quiet study and reflection ranges from 10% to 100% of the total space they are providing for faculty and graduate students, with a mean of 73%. Nineteen respondents report that louder collaborative work spaces ranges from 5% to

100% of their total, but the average amount of space devoted to this use is significantly smaller, about 33%. The percentage allocation of space for other purposes is too small to be useful to the study.

Services Provided

Thirty-six libraries responded to the set of questions on which technology services are provided to faculty and grad students. Although a few institutions maintain study spaces without technology, the vast majority (32 of 36 or 89%) provide access to computers, either desktop or loaning laptops. Seven institutions provide both desktop and laptop computers for the use of both faculty and graduate students. Of the others, 17 provide desktop computers and 11 provide laptops. Reproduction equipment, display surfaces, and computer peripherals are the next most frequently provided technologies, and this equipment is rarely for the exclusive use of either faculty or grad students. Software workshops or assistance are provided by 39% of respondents (14 institutions), with most reporting that both user groups are offered this service. A surprising number of institutions (11 or 31%) reported staff-mediated services for printing and scanning; eight of these (22%) also offer staff-mediated digitization.

Most of the research support offered to these populations by the 27 responding institutions are standard library services. The overwhelming majority (26 or 96%) offer reference or research help, whether remote, from a service desk, or by appointment; 48% offer all three of these options. Of the nine institutions that choose to offer only one type of reference service, eight provide remote reference/research help and one offers appointment-based help. Sixteen institutions offer either numeric data or GIS services; 11 of these offer both. Citation management software and assistance is widely offered (20 institutions or 74%), and only four limit this service exclusively to one group or the other.

A few institutions provide services that are more unique. One offers services for organizing conferences and colloquiums, one organizes and publicizes talks by experts, and another coordinates a graduate student workshop series. Several respondents also mentioned media support.

Seventeen of the responding institutions offer teaching support services, most (14 or 82%) offer instructional skills workshops and assistance; only one of these limits this service to faculty. Eleven institutions (65%) offer both instructional skills and educational technology workshops, and six of these also offer learning object creation workshops, indicating there is synergy in this combination of services. Six institutions offer video conferencing services and four of them also provide vodcasting and podcasting; three others offer podcasting only.

Eighteen institutions reported offering personal growth services (personal counselling, dissertation completion support, writing clinic, etc.) to graduate students and faculty in library service spaces. Traditional library information literacy/bibliographic instruction sessions are most common, but it is surprising that this category was not more widely reported—only 15 of the 37 libraries that answered service questions indicated that they are providing information literacy or bibliographic instruction for grad students and faculty. Comments suggested that more institutions are offering personal growth services, but not exclusively to these populations. Four institutions offer both academic content development and writing/editing services in combination. One institution offers special services to international graduate students.

Partnerships

Forty-four institutions responded to the set of questions about partnering with other campus units to provide services to faculty and graduate students. Thirty-one (70%) indicated that they partner with at least one campus unit; 13 reported no such partnerships. Twenty-seven of the 31 (87%) partner with at least the campus computing center. Of the other four, one partners with the writing center and office of research; one partners with the faculty development/teaching excellence office and the graduate student development office; another partners with faculty development, grad student development, and the writing center; the fourth reported that it's sole partnership is with the office of research for grant writing. Eight respondents report that their sole partnership is with campus computing. The other 19 have partnerships with campus computing and at least two other campus units; 16 maintain partnerships with four or more campus units. In addition to the six categories of partners included in the survey, respondents mentioned other partners, including the Provost, Study Partners tutoring service, Intercollegiate Athletics, the Art Department, the Office of Campus-Community Engagement, Services for Students with Disabilities, Career Services, and campus food services.

Overwhelmingly, these partnerships are informal, without contracts or Memorandums of Understanding (MOUs). Most formal agreements are made with campus computing, where eight institutions document some arrangements and two institutions document all arrangements. One institution noted that an MOU is in place with the Learning Technologies office for some shared classrooms, and another reported that some arrangements with the writing center are documented. No written agreements were reported with Faculty Development offices, Graduate Studies, and the Offices of Research. Several institutions commented that they have a partnership with the campus writing center, but that no services are provided specifically for faculty and/or graduate students.

Service Point Staffing

Ten institutions reported on staff working at service points specifically designated for graduate students and/or faculty. Overall, the results show that presently very few staff members are dedicated to providing services for faculty and graduate students. The lowest staffing level reported was one individual and the highest was 60, with an average staffing complement of 13.5. Seven of the respondents reported between one and eight individuals (for an average of 4.9). The respondent that reported roughly 16 staff provides services in renovated space, the Digital Social Science Center, within a branch library. The respondent that reported 25 staff provides services in the Faculty Commons within the main library. The library that

reported the highest number of staff (60) explained, "A planned renovation of the first two floors of the main library will be referred to as the Knowledge Commons. The new Knowledge Commons will include a new Center for Faculty Excellence."

Nine institutions identified a director or coordinator position specifically responsible for overseeing spaces and/or services for graduate students and/or faculty. Of the position titles supplied, only one appears to be a position exclusively dedicated to these researchers (Head of Graduate Services). All other position titles seem to indicate a broader responsibility, including faculty and grad services with other more general services.

In all but a few cases, libraries and their partners used a combination of strategies to fill staff positions. Seven of 11 libraries redefined job descriptions of existing staff, four of which were reassigned. Four of the seven also created new positions, as did two libraries' partners. In another case, the library and its partner both reassigned staff. In yet another, the partner alone redefined and reassigned staff. In only two cases did the library and/or its partner simply create a new position.

Marketing/Outreach

The majority of respondents (33 of 41 respondents or 80%) indicated that they do not have a formal marketing plan in place to promote spaces and services for faculty and graduate students. Several mentioned that these services are included in their overall marketing strategy and others indicated that promotion for these services is in the planning stages.

Word of mouth is the most frequently reported method of promoting these spaces and services (used by 93% of respondents), but most institutions do not rely on this strategy alone. Only one institution said: "… we purposefully depend only on word of mouth and do not market their availability. There is always a waiting list for these spaces." An equal number of institutions (28 or 68%) use the library Web site, printed literature, such as brochures and bookmarks, and faculty and graduate student orientation sessions as ways of reaching these groups. Visits to faculty and graduate student meetings and targeted e-mail announcements are also frequently used. On average, libraries are using more than five marketing strategies in combination, with a few institutions (5 of 40) using all of the traditional methods included in the survey. In addition to these methods, several institutions also mentioned more innovative marketing strategies, such as separate research commons Web sites, plasma screens in a Faculty Commons, public computer screen savers, office hours in departmental offices, specific identification on building floorplans and signage, receptions, and Facebook ads for grad students.

Statistics and Assessment

A surprising number of institutions (32%) do not keep any statistics on graduate student and/or faculty use of spaces and services. Of the institutions that do keep track, most use one or more of the fairly traditional methods of quantifying library services, such as session counts, head and gate counts, and questions answered. Only seven institutions reported using Web or print comments, another traditional library method of gathering user feedback. Comments revealed that at least six institutions monitor space use by recording carrel and room bookings or access cards issued. Two institutions record document delivery service use. One institution indicated that they monitor grants received and another "statements in dissertations."

Most libraries use some method for evaluating faculty and graduate student satisfaction with their spaces and services. A surprisingly low number (6 of 41 respondents) make no formal assessment efforts. A large number (63%) participate in LibQUAL+®. Only two institutions rely on LibQUAL+® alone; most use it in conjunction with one or more additional methods of assessment. Most of the assessment methods employed are voluntary and, other than LibQUAL+®, solicit opinions from users rather than non-users of library services. Most of the satisfaction measures in use are qualitative and fairly traditional. Only one institution indicated participation in a broad-based research study.

Conclusion

Clearly, ARL libraries continue to experiment with a variety of space and service models to support the teaching, learning, and research needs of faculty and graduate students on their campuses. The new models are being triggered by a variety of forces — most notably by explicit requests from graduate students and, to a lesser extent, faculty themselves. Survey respondents have adopted a variety of instruments for gathering input into space and service design but have, to date, relied fairly heavily on anecdotal feedback.

Many sites support a relatively traditional buffet of spaces — but have repackaged them in new ways for this targeted population. Virtually all sites provide the standard library spaces (e.g., study seating, lounge seating, and collaborative study), but in many cases, have allocated discrete areas for their faculty and graduate students. The non-traditional offerings run the full gamut — from fully-equipped classrooms to 3D visualization spaces.

The service models also vary considerably. The reported models feature a strong emphasis on traditional services (reference/research help, interlibrary loan, etc.) — but again reimaged to meet the distinct needs of faculty and graduate students. The services support a heavy emphasis on technology. A significant number of ARL libraries are providing teaching support services within their spaces. Few sites are providing personal growth services (personal counselling, dissertation completion support, writing clinic, etc.) — other than the traditional information literacy sessions.

During this development phase, many sites are adopting flexible approaches: spaces and services are designed with faculty and graduate students in mind — but other populations are often allowed to use them under some circumstances.

Sites report relationships with multiple partners — most often their campus computing unit and, to a lesser extent, their faculty development/teaching excellence office. The small number of sites reporting relationships with other campus units (e.g., graduate student development offices, writing centers, research office) was surprising. The lack of formal documentation for these partnerships was a point of concern.

ARL member libraries employ a variety of instruments for publicizing their spaces and services for this population — but very few have formal marketing plans. Very few keep discrete statistics or evaluate their deliverables beyond the traditional general library assessment tools.

Further research is required to determine the success of these new services and spaces over time. Still to be discovered are how satisfied users are with the new offerings, how sustainable the new service models will be over time, and ultimately, what impact these new deliverables will have on the teaching, learning, and research conducted by faculty and graduate students.

SURVEY QUESTIONS AND RESPONSES

The SPEC survey on Graduate Student and Faculty Spaces and Services was designed by **Vivian Lewis**, Associate University Librarian, Organizational Analysis, Planning & Accountability, and **Cathy Moulder**, Director of Library Services, Maps, Data & GIS, McMaster University. These results are based on data submitted by 65 of the 123 ARL member libraries (53%) by the deadline of May 2, 2008. The survey's introductory text and questions are reproduced below, followed by the response data and selected comments from the respondents.

Over the last decade, research libraries have focused increasing attention on serving the needs of the undergraduate student. In many cases, large collection areas have been converted into learning or information commons facilities—complete with vast banks of public computers, collaborative study rooms, comfortable furnishings, and relaxed noise, food, and drink regulations. Some have incorporated a wide spectrum of student-centered services, including writing centers, academic skills counselling, tutoring services, and more.

In many cases, faculty and graduate students are welcome to use these spaces and services but are not considered the primary customers. As faculty and graduate students observe these transformations, they are inspired to ask their libraries if the same attention will be turned to their needs.

Recently, ARL libraries have begun to experiment with an enriched set of spaces and services to meet the complex teaching, learning, and research needs of graduate students and faculty. Some libraries have introduced small sanctuaries (study rooms or lounges) for graduate students and faculty as distinctly separate from undergraduate spaces. Others are providing new suites of services like dissertation support, curriculum design, and learning object design. In some cases, the services are offered in collaboration with other campus units—perhaps the Faculty Development Office, the Learning Technology Office, or Campus Computing. The new services and spaces may be localized in a discrete area (sometimes called a "research commons" or "faculty commons") or opportunistically distributed across the library system.

This survey is designed to explore the variety of resources and services being delivered or envisioned specifically for faculty and/or graduate students, the location(s) of service delivery, service point staffing, partners in service delivery, marketing of services, and assessment of the use of these spaces and services.

BACKGROUND

1. Does your library provide (or plan to provide) spaces or services specifically designed for graduate students and/or faculty? N=65

We provide (or plan to provide) spaces or services specifically designed for **both graduate students and faculty**	39	60%
We provide (or plan to provide) spaces or services specifically designed for **graduate students** but not faculty	7	10%
We provide (or plan to provide) spaces or services specifically designed for **faculty** but not graduate students	2	3%
We don't distinguish between spaces or services for graduate students or faculty and other users	14	22%
Not applicable, this is not an academic library	3	5%

If your library provides (or plans to provide) spaces or services specifically designed for graduate students and/or faculty, please complete this survey.

If your library doesn't distinguish between spaces or services for graduate students or faculty and other users, or is not an academic library, submit the survey now. Thank you—your response is also valuable.

2. What drove the decision to provide spaces or services specifically designed for graduate students and/or faculty? Check all that apply. N=48

	N	Graduate Students	Faculty	Both
		31	19	36
Requests from graduate students	33	27	—	6
Building renovation/reorganization	25	11	1	13
Requests from faculty	23	3	15	5
Result of a strategic planning process	23	5	3	15
Recommendations from library staff	21	5	—	16
Independent decision by the library administration	16	4	1	11
Influenced by success of other institutions	9	2	—	7
Funding opportunity specified these services	6	—	3	3
Independent decision by a group of campus units including the library	4	—	2	2
Funding opportunity specified this space	2	—	1	1
Mandated by an external body	—	—	—	—
Other reason	23	9	1	13

Please describe other reason(s).

Graduate Students

"A special 'Graduate Services' Library has existed for many decades at Berkeley, though a relocation and redesign of the space occurred about 10 years ago. There are other locations with special services for graduate students as well."

"Focus groups when planning new space in Biomedical Library."

"In consultation with Dean, Graduate Studies."

"Ours is a widely distributed library system. A number of professional school libraries have study rooms and facilities that are intended to be available only to the professional or graduate students affiliated with that school."

"Results of user surveys and focus groups showing that grad students have very different needs. Planned increase in the grad student population by the university--potentially 1,400 grad students. Benchmarking seating at similar university libraries."

"Separate spaces for faculty and graduate students have been provided since the initial building was constructed in the 1960s. Separate spaces were maintained after the building was renovated in 2004 though in different formats."

"The student interest was discovered as part of our Mellon-funded study on the research needs of faculty and grad students."

"Through repeated comments/suggestions in the LibQUAL+ surveys."

"We had a similar space but it was in great need of improvements."

Faculty

"Influenced by success of Learning Commons with undergraduate students."

Both

"Initiated as a complement to Undergraduate Learning Commons."

"Opportunity to collaborate with the Director of Teaching and Learning who reports to the Vice-Provost (Academic Programs and Students). The Teaching Support Centre (TSC) moved into newly renovated space in The D.B. Weldon Library which is centrally located on campus. The Information Literacy Librarian, who reports to the Associate University Librarian (Planning and Services) has an office in the TSC, works with the TSC staff and provides information literacy leadership in the Libraries."

"Our spaces specifically for faculty + graduate students are limited to research study carrels which were part of the original design plan for the main library building which opened in 1970. We have classroom spaces that faculty can use on a limited basis for classes. At one time we had a document delivery service for books for faculty, but that was discontinued several years ago. So I expect I may find it difficult to answer this survey."

"Our study spaces and carrels for grad students and faculty have been available for a number of years."

"Result of space planning process within the libraries. Space will be become available with the construction of a second module as part of our off-site storage facility. In addition, central campus space is at a premium and use of library space to consolidate and create services for faculty and graduate services in one location is central to our planning for the Research Commons."

"Study spaces for faculty and graduate students have been available at the Bizzell Memorial Library (main library) for more than 30 years."

"The recent opening of the new Irving K. Barber Learning Centre (official opening was held April 11, 2008) provides the opportunity for planning new programs and services for all users, graduates students and faculty included. The IKBLC, University of British Columbia Library: 200,000 square feet of new space and more than 46,000 square feet of renovated space. Includes innovative learning spaces, including a 157-set theatre, new technologies, flexible furniture to support large and small space work; breakout rooms, an array of seminar/study rooms and classrooms, for groups ranging from 6 to 110 people. Onsite webcasting and video-conferencing capabilities, simulation and gaming technologies for learning support. Office space and study spaces for UBC's School of Library, Archival and Information Studies, officers and other facilities for the Centre for Teaching and Academic Growth (TAG), media commons, learning commons, etc. Potential partnerships with student development office, Office of Learning Technology, Writing Centre, TAG, and more. And, of course, a Library with the Chapman Learning Commons, and other reference/instruction/outreach/liaison services."

"The success of the Information Commons made us realize that we needed to provide better space for all of our Clientel and began investigating what other institutions were doing in this area."

"Tradition of providing services/spaces to faculty and graduate students."

"We have a graduate student reading room, individual closed study carrels for graduate students, and individual closed study carrels for faculty. They have been in place since the building was built in 1970."

"We have a satellite campus library that was designed to serve faculty and students in executive graduate programs."

"We have historically provided spaces for both faculty and grad students. Recently we have recognized the need to rethink the space and to identify complementary services. At the same time we have been approached by the Graduate College (on behalf of students) with a request for some space specifically where dissertation writing groups can meet. So basic space currently being provided for both group, but looking at providing different/better space and services for grad students."

"We have provided Faculty & Graduate reading rooms in both our main library and science library for a number of years. In the main library, the reading room is for use by both faculty and grad students. In the Science Library, we used to provide two reading rooms — one for Faculty and one for Grad students. However, we have recently consolidated into a combined faculty/grad student reading room."

3. Are spaces or services targeted to a specific department or discipline? N=47

	Yes	No
Graduate Students	13	34
Faculty	8	33
Total number of respondents	13	36

If yes, please specify the department(s) or discipline(s).

"Art History, Music, Faculty study spaces in Humanities and Social Sciences."

"Business; Law School."

"Digital Humanities projects, faculty and graduate students."

"Education, Business Administration, Information Sciences, and select engineering programs and research institutes."

"Faculties of: Science & Engineering; Agriculture & Environmental Sciences; Arts."

"For Graduate Study Room: targeted to School of Medicine and Division of Biological Sciences but is open to all graduate students in any discipline. For graduate student lockers: targeted to any graduate student using the arts collections."

"Graduate Services Library focuses mainly on the humanities, though welcomes all. Data Lab focuses mainly on the social sciences, though welcomes all."

"Humanities and Social Sciences."

"Humanities and Social Sciences, Asia Studies."

"Humanities and social sciences; Science: Astronomy, chemistry, biology/psychology, physics; Fine Arts: art history, architecture, drama; Music; Education. Also administratively separate law, health sciences, and graduate business."

"Humanities, social sciences, health sciences."

"Social Sciences and Humanities disciplines for both faculty and graduate student spaces; graduate student spaces in all disciplines."

"Social Sciences departments."

4. Please indicate which of the individuals, groups, or entities below the library contacted, and by what means, to gather information about the space(s) or services to offer. Check all that apply. N=43

	N	Faculty representative(s)	Student representative(s)	Library staff	Other libraries	Campus computing unit representative(s)	Student support services representative(s)	Consultants	Faculty development office representative(s)	Other individuals, group, or entity
	N	36	35	33	21	13	8	7	6	8
Anecdotal feedback/informal conversations	34	22	22	27	13	6	3	—	3	2
Focus groups	20	11	17	3	—	1	2	—	—	2
Surveys	19	15	18	6	—	2	2	—	—	—
Field observations	17	5	6	11	7	—	—	2	2	1
Formal interviews with constituent groups	16	10	13	4	1	4	—	1	2	2
Expert opinion	14	8	3	6	5	5	2	4	3	2
Other information gathering method	9	5	4	—	3	—	—	—	—	—

Please describe the other individuals, group, or entity.

Please describe the other information gathering method and the corresponding individuals, group, or entity.

Other individual(s), group(s), or entity contacted.	Other information gathering method and the corresponding individuals, group, or entity.	Comments
Before renovation we had focus groups with graduate students and also talked with faculty representatives about proposed changes in spaces for these two groups.	Prior to renovation we visited other libraries and looked at spaces they provided for these groups.	Prior to renovation we had individual faculty carrels on all floors. We now have individual faculty carrels on the two lower floors and group faculty carrels on the two upper floors. We had very small individual graduate carrels on the floors before renovation; we now have group graduate carrels on the floors. All carrels are card-accessible via their ID cards.
Deans (expert opinion)	LibQUAL+®	
Department chairs		Some of the study rooms have been in existence for decades, so the methodology for their development is unknown.
Director of Teaching and Learning Centre, Campus Master Plan Committee (expert opinion)		
Entire campus was surveyed in 2002, 2005 by LibQUAL+®.		
Faculty and grad students in a variety of departments across campus participated in both our Humanities/ Social Sciences study and the subsequent sciences assessment. We heard the desire for grad study space from the humanities / social sciences group, but not from the sciences group.		

Other individual(s), group(s), or entity contacted.	Other information gathering method and the corresponding individuals, group, or entity.	Comments
Graduate and faculty tours and orientations. Current holders of spaces in Olin, the library currently in design development for a phased renovation. (formal interviews)	Field observation in general for student study spaces. Interviews.	
Most of the communication regarding these spaces comes through representatives to the library via formal campus committees.	Comments from LibQUAL+® have been helpful in obtaining feedback about these spaces.	
Non-library staff at our university; Members of the public who are not affiliated with our university but who use the library; University alumni; Donors to the library and to the university. (anecdotal feedback)	Meetings of standing faculty committees—formal and informal conversations; University library donors—informal conversations; University alumni—informal conversations.	
Other libraries where an information commons has been implemented.	infocommons-l listserv	The listserv has been incredibly helpful.
Our satellite campus was modeled on corporate libraries.		
Staff of the student union on Grounds. (focus groups)		
The Dean's office (having previously been contacted by students) strongly supported the development of many additional group study rooms in the Owen Library renovation.		
The library has provided study carrels for graduate students for about 20 years.		
Data support group (not connected to campus computing), Institute for Governmental Studies, Survey Research Center. (anecdotal feedback)		Since we have several spaces and services specifically for graduate students, it is difficult to summarize all in one list. It is also challenging since many of these spaces/services were conceived and in place prior to my arrival on campus and I do not have a complete history to reference.

Other individual(s), group(s), or entity contacted.	Other information gathering method and the corresponding individuals, group, or entity.	Comments
VP Academic; individual conversations/complaints by graduate students; informal conversations from faculty; comments on LibQUAL+®	Meetings/correspondence with administrative faculty	
We have met with the Provost, the College of Arts and Sciences Policy Committee, the Dean and Executive Associate Dean of the College, the Bloomington Faculty Council Library Committee, the Dean and Associate Dean of the Graduate School, the Associate Vice Provost for Research and the Associate Provosts for Research. So far, only graduate students have been included in focus groups.		
	Focus groups: medical and pharmacy students primarily.	
	Input from faculty development office staff included feedback gathered from a Faculty Development Advisory Committee.	This project was planned jointly with staff from most of the units eventually housed in the Faculty Commons. Each participating unit had been actively gathering information from faculty for some time before we developed the idea of locating these services together in the library.
	LibQUAL+® survey, 2007. Graduate students and faculty user groups. We identified needs (in general) and in specific disciplines/library branches and follow up is still required to convert the needs into the operational plans and programs.	
	The Library did not contact others, campus IT did.	

Other individual(s), group(s), or entity contacted.	Other information gathering method and the corresponding individuals, group, or entity.	Comments
	We conducted a number of site visits to other academic libraries.	
	We contacted the Graduate Student Council about dedicating space for graduate and faculty quiet study.	
	We met in late March with a representative group of graduate students, toured our Main Library with them, talked about the spaces that we are currently providing, and solicited ideas on what they would like to see in Main Library. Though specifically a conversation about space, we did touch on services that might be beneficial for this population.	In addition, in January, a library group was charged with identifying the necessary and desired components of a cohesive program for providing information skills instruction to graduate students. This endeavor is also shaping some of our thinking as we move forward with this.

Additional Comments

"As indicated in earlier comment, graduate students comments in LibQUAL+ survey the need for their own library space."

"The small amount of space (private study carrels in a quiet zone) has been in place for many, many years."

"We are not even to this stage. We are just thinking about what should be in our area and will be gathering our data in the next year or so."

"We have a graduate study center in the largest of our six libraries. The space was designated for this use back in 1994 when the addition opened. No one recalls any particular process that was used. The graduate school and the grad student association handles the staffing. It's mostly a computer lab with some meeting space. No library connection beyond them being in our space. As for faculty, we had a request from central admin to house an Emeritus Faculty facility; it is housed in our science library in a space that had been vacant for years. They remodeled at their cost. They have meeting spaces, individual offices that faculty can use, and office space for the program director and secretary. They are just getting this program off the ground and will likely be offering other services that will be coordinated by their staff."

"We have just initiated a planning process to evaluate our current space use and needs. We will likely utilize all the methods noted above in developing our plans."

"When deciding to combine faculty & grad student reading rooms in the science library, we reviewed usage statistics, conducted focus groups with grad students, and contacted faculty who were heavy users of the faculty reading room."

5. Please indicate whether any of the factors below influenced the library's thinking about the space(s) or services to offer. Check all that apply. N=36

		Graduate Students	Faculty	Both
	N	10	5	25
Site visits	19	6	1	12
Literature searches	19	4	1	14
Expert opinion	19	3	1	15
Presentations attended at conferences	18	2	1	15
Funded research	7	1	2	4
Other	8	2	2	4

Please specify other factor(s).

Graduate Students

"Library staff initiative, along with observed success at other libraries."

"Libraries felt lockers would be a good service given that we did not have assignable carrels nor a room/space that could be dedicated for/restricted to graduate students."

Faculty

"Information from EDUCAUSE Learning Space Design Constituent Group."

"Visual checks by library staff on the use of these carrels (prior to renovation)."

Both

"Onsite observation of users' behavior; Data on library use (gathered by our library)."

"Developments were made in the past 10 years to accommodate more electronic access and services."

"LibQUAL+® survey comments that were received back in 2001."

"Observed how use of the facility has changed over time as more resources are electronic and as we deliver more information to the desk top. The campus is undergoing a master planning process and one theme that has emerged is providing spaces that foster a sense of community, whether as a whole or with groups such as faculty and graduate students. The library is considering what kinds of spaces and services will build community between these two groups."

Other

"Available spaces. Funding. Mellon grant stipulations."

"Specific plans/programs and strategies will be explored in May 2008 with the on-site visit of the ARL Program Officers, who will consult with us on an Effective, Sustainable and Practical Library Assessment program. This program will include services to graduate students and faculty."

Additional Comments

"Our Learning Commons, like many others in academic libraries, is heavily populated with undergraduates. Yet we also know that graduate students use the collections intensively and may not have other space on campus in which to work."

"Site visits are planned to other libraries."

"We are interested in creating a space similar to the one for faculty at Valparaiso University where faculty are given a group office, any may use it, but each academic year a faculty member is selected to use the office as their permanent office and is then responsible for developing programming for other faculty."

"We have a strong partnership with our central computing organization and partnering with them figures prominently in our planning."

SERVICE LOCATION(S)

6. Which of the following best describes the location(s) for the delivery of services specifically designed for graduate students and/or faculty? N=42

	N	Graduate Students	Faculty	Both
		10	4	32
Services are delivered from pre-existing service points	20	4	—	16
Services are consolidated in a single discrete location (e.g., a research commons)	18	3	4	11
Services are dispersed across several new service points or locations	14	3	—	11
Other	8	2	—	6

Please specify other location(s).

Graduate Students

"Document delivery for graduate students is requested online, but delivered at a pre-existing service point."

"Lockers are provided in space in the Arts Libraries. Graduate Study Room is in our Biomedical Library."

Both

"Coordination of distributed campus support services through Web site."

"The services provided are faculty studies or graduate carrels; these are small spaces (sometimes shared) with a desk, chair, Internet connection, and bookcase."

"Two graduate student study rooms in bookstacks tower of main library. Still in planning stages for new faculty spaces. 65 faculty research study rooms are available for assignment upon request."

"Western Libraries: services are delivered from pre-existing service points. Teaching Support Centre is newer and in one location in The D.B. Weldon Library. Proposed that there will be library services delivery in newly planned campus community spaces."

Other

"Faculty individual studies have been improved with wireless and new furniture."

"Humanities and social sciences; Science: Astronomy, chemistry, biology/psychology, physics; Fine Arts: art history, architecture, drama; Music; Education."

"Reading rooms and reference desks; access and circulation services desks; study commons; information desks."

"The Library core (heritage part) is pre-existing but renovated. The Irving K. Barber Learning Centre is built around the heritage core and adds to new wings, one of which is the Library, one of which houses the wide range of learning spaces, classrooms, social spaces, etc."

"The University of Delaware Library provides Faculty Research Studies for individual faculty research use, approved by application to a Faculty Committee. The Library also provides graduate research carrels with locked storage area for research materials that are each shared by two graduate students. The Library also provides a Retired Faculty research room that provides a location for a small group of faculty to do research, use a computer, printer, and fax machine."

"We have only a modest beginning with one large group study room in one library designated for graduate student use."

"We provide some services to departments by holding office hours within certain departments."

Additional Comments

"Offer new spaces, not new services."

"Research commons is in the planning stages. Right now we have the Learning Commons which provides consultation services for faculty/graduate students and spaces. Additional rooms have been set up elsewhere in the building to provide different types of dedicated spaces for these groups."

"The faculty service here is the 'Faculty Delivery service' that delivers books to the faculty member's office and/or articles delivered via e-mail. This campus-wide service is coordinated and staffed out of the Interlibrary Loan office."

"The Research Commons will consist of 9 floors in the Wells Library. Space will be remodeled over time and will include new service points and new partners."

"We are still providing services for faculty and grad students as a component of our overall service delivery."

"We do not staff the faculty and graduate student reading rooms. Other services are provided to faculty and grad students at pre-existing service points."

SERVICE POINT DESCRIPTION

7. Please provide the name(s) (or a brief description if there is no name) of the space(s) where services are delivered. N=38

    See table below.

8. In which building(s) is the service point(s) located? Check all that apply. N=43

Within the main campus library	39	91%
Within a branch library	19	44%
In a non-library building on campus	4	9%
Other building	2	5%

Please specify the name and/or discipline of the branch library. N=17

Please specify the name and/or discipline of the non-library building. N=3

Please specify the other building. N=2

Name/description	Main campus library	Branch library	Non-library building	Other building	Comments
A planned renovation of the first two floors of the main library will be referred to as the Knowledge Commons. The new Knowledge Commons will include a new Center for Faculty Excellence.	✔				
Carrels and group study room in Wilson Library, our largest library with materials for arts, humanities, social sciences.	✔				
Digital Media Lab; Chalk Learning Management System Office	✔				
Faculty Commons	✔				
Faculty Research Studies, Graduate Research Carrels, Retired Faculty Research Room	✔				
Faculty studies; graduate student carrels	✔				
Faculty Study Rooms; Scholar Study Rooms	✔				
Faculty support center; visualization lab	✔				
Graduate Services	✔				
Graduate Student and Faculty Quiet Study Area	✔				
Graduate student floor, graduate and faculty carrels	✔				
Graduate Student Study Suite	✔				
Graduate Student Success Center	✔				
Graduate Study Room	✔				

Name/description	Main campus library	Branch library	Non-library building	Other building	Comments
Individual study rooms	✔				
Kelvin Smith Library	✔				
Learning Commons service desk	✔				This is what we currently have--a planning process will determine how much segmentation of service points will be needed when we are able to offer more customized spaces.
Scholarly Commons	✔				
Service: document delivery for graduate students, delivered at circulation desk	✔				
Student Multimedia Studio, Presentation Practice Room	✔				
Unspecified	✔				
Unspecified	✔				
William T. Young Library	✔				
Information Desk	✔	13 branches			
Graduate reading rooms, faculty study areas, graduate carrels at music and art libraries	✔	Art library, Music library, Douglass library			
Libraries for humanities and social sciences, science, Astronomy, chemistry, biology/psychology, physics, fine arts, music, education	✔	Humanities and social sciences, science, Astronomy, chemistry, biology/ psychology, physics, fine arts, music, education			

Name/description	Main campus library	Branch library	Non-library building	Other building	Comments
Quiet Study Floors and Faculty Writing Place	✔	Integrated Sciences and Engineering Library: quiet study space			Quiet Study Rooms: These are rooms that have wireless and comfortable individual study spaces. Quiet is enforced through User Behavior Policies and building monitors. Faculty Writing Place: This is a room specifically for faculty to drop in and writing alone or in groups. Faculty development workshops are held here as well. Begun with a Mellon grant. Hosted collaboratively between the Library and Office of Faculty Development
Roger C. Holden Faculty and Graduate Student Reading Room; Science Library Faculty and Graduate Reading Room	✔	Science Library			
Olin Library, Kroch Library, Mann Library	✔	See comment.			Olin and Kroch libraries are separate libraries but function as one library and while Cornell does not have a 'main' library, for this purpose Olin/Kroch would represent the main library because of its size, use and home for the library administration. Mann Library would represent a branch library.

Name/description	Main campus library	Branch library	Non-library building	Other building	Comments
Access Desk; Circulation Desk; Reference Desk; Microfilm & Microfiche Room; Interlibrary Loan; Maps and Government Information; CLICC Lab; subject libraries for Arts, Music, Medicine, sciences, Management, undergraduates	✔	SEL (Science & Engineering Library); College Library; Biomedical Library; Management Library; Music Library; Arts Library; Young Research Library			
Reference Desk and Library Training Room	✔	Veterinary Medicine			New workshops were held both in the main building and in the Veterinary Medicine library which services a program that consists solely of graduate students.
Research Commons: to be located in the east tower in the Wells Library	✔	We are considering the creation of a science-focused library from three existing subject-specific libraries. It will include statistics and GIS support near science faculty and graduate students.			
Unspecified	✔	The branch library is housed in the branch campus building.			

Name/description	Main campus library	Branch library	Non-library building	Other building	Comments
Unspecified	✔	Unspecified			Again, services are not separated out.
Unspecified	✔	Unspecified			We have a special graduate study room which contains some computer workstations and a printing area. The rest of our services are not specific to graduate students but are offered in tandem with other services.
Service desks in all libraries; Teaching Support Centre	✔	Teaching Support Centre is located in The D.B. Weldon Library (Arts and Humanities, Information & Media Studies, and Social Sciences)	Service desks located in: Business, Education, Law, Music, Allyn & Betty Taylor (Engineering, Health Sciences, Medicine & Dentistry and Science) and The D.B. Weldon libraries and Western Archives,		
Faculty offices / graduate study carrels	✔	Various	Departmental offices		
Web	✔	Unspecified	Unspecified		

Name/description	Main campus library	Branch library	Non-library building	Other building	Comments
Graduate Student Computer Cluster	✔	Rockefeller Library - main humanities and social sciences library	Sciences Library	Librarian in the Lobby: collections librarian has office hours in academic buildings.	
Digital Social Science Center		Lehman Library for the Social Sciences			
Graduate Study Room; Lockers for graduate students.		Biomedical Library and the Arts Libraries (2 buildings).			
Study Rooms: Business School Library		Owen Management School Library			
Chapman Learning Commons				The Irving K. Barber Learning Centre is a library, a branch library (in some respects), and a learning centre.	

9. Is the service point(s) in renovated or newly constructed space? N=30

Renovated space	23	77%
A combination of renovated and newly constructed space	7	23%
Newly constructed space	—	—

Comments

Renovated Space

"Biomedical Library Graduate Study Room."

"Library facilities were renovated in 2006. No additional space was added, collection stack space was transformed to user space."

"Renovated about a decade ago."

"Some of the subject-specific spaces have been renovated within the last several years."

"The group room had been staff offices. When offices were removed, we painted and put in new carpet and furniture."

"Will be renovated in next 18 months; part of Learning Commons project."

Combination

"Depends on the building."

"The Irving K. Barber Learning Centre houses Rare Books & Special Collections, University Archives, Fine Arts Library, Science & Engineering Division ('library' spaces). It also houses the Chapman Learning Commons, a multi-use service point, both library information services and student services. Possibly also information technology support (tbd). IKBLC also houses a host of flexible classrooms, study rooms, media rooms, social spaces, and quiet study spaces."

"The Teaching Support Centre is in a renovated space in The D.B. Weldon Library. Some service desks in the libraries have been redesigned."

"The University purchased an older building and renovated it for academic purposes."

Other

"It's a space that badly needs renovation and future renovation plans will develop some much improved spaces for faculty and grad students."

"The faculty and graduate student reading rooms are not new. We have provided these services for a number of years."

"The spaces are not service points."

10. Are patrons other than graduate students and/or faculty allowed to use the service point(s)?
    N=39

Yes	26	67%
No	13	33%

If yes, please specify who else may use the service point(s).

"All."

"All patrons with circulation privileges use the circulation desk."

"Any library user."

"Any Virginia citizen 16 years and older."

"Anyone with valid university ID."

"Community."

"Faculty."

"Faculty _cannot_ use these spaces. They are however open to _both_ undergraduates and graduate students."

"Faculty are the primary users of services offered by the units housed within the Faculty Commons, but we also welcome any student or administrative staff member with need of these services. Graduate student instructors use the services of the Center for Teaching and Learning, for example."

"Faculty Writing Place is only for faculty. Quiet Study space is for all."

"If carrels are not occupied others may sit at them."

"In some spaces the response would be 'yes' and in some 'no.'"

"Members of the general public; undergraduates; students and faculty from other institutions not enrolled here."

"Only in the case of a seminar room that may be reserved by faculty; others may use the space but may not reserve it and must give it up when faculty wish to use it."

"Service points were not specifically created for faculty or graduate students."

"Staff/students authorized on their behalf."

"The new Center for Faculty Excellence will primarily serve faculty and graduate students, but the other service points in the Knowledge Commons will be open and available to undergraduates. Some, but not all of the services and spaces will be open to non-affiliated researchers."

"The Roger C. Holden Faculty and Graduate Student Reading Room is typically reserved for faculty and grad students, but it is occasionally used for events and presentations that are open to a wider audience. The Science Library Faculty and Graduate Student Reading Room is always reserved for faculty and grad students."

"The service at the library service desks is available to all users. While this is the case, there are services designed for graduate students and faculty to meet their research and teaching needs. For example, graduate students and faculty can make appointments with librarians/archivists for in-depth archival and research support. The Teaching Support Centre is for faculty and graduate students only."

"The service point is open to anyone that wants to avail themselves of our services."

"This branch is open to the public and used by a small undergraduate class as well as other students and faculty who live near the campus."

"Undergraduates and staff."

"Undergraduates will be allowed to use the visualization lab."

"Visiting scholars. As we develop additional services, we will not restrict undergrad use."

11. How many hours per week is the service point(s) open? N=29

Hours per week

Minimum	Maximum	Mean	Median	Std Dev
40	168	105	102	34.73

12. To whom does the service point(s) report? Check all that apply. N=40

Library director/dean	30	75%
Provost	3	8%
Academic department dean	1	3%
Campus advisory committee	1	3%
Office of Research	—	—
Other	13	33%

Please specify other.

Associate Dean in University Library

Associate University Librarian

AUL for Access Services

Both Library Director and IKBLC Director

Center for Academic Technology reports to CIO

CIO

Director of Social Science Libraries

Director of Teaching and Learning

Director of the Owen Library

Head of access services

Head of branch library

Individual Research Study Rooms are managed by the Stacks Supervisor

Senior Director, NSIT Academic Technologies (Note: NSIT stands for Networking Services and Information Technologies, and is the computer organization on the campus)

Additional Comments

"All 3 libraries ultimately report to the Provost. Olin and Kroch report to the University Librarian. Mann Library reports both to the University Librarian and a Dean."

"Faculty studies are renewed every two years; graduate student carrels are renewed every year."

13. Which kinds of physical environments are available in the service space(s)? Check all that apply. N=41

	N	Graduate Students	Faculty	Both
		14	6	33
Study seating (individual/quiet study)	37	6	2	29
Lounge seating	24	9	2	13
Collaborative rooms	18	6	3	9
Meeting space	16	2	3	10
Service desk	14	2	1	11
Space for socializing	12	1	2	9
Recording/videotaping room	10	1	1	8
Training spaces distinctly separate from classrooms	9	—	2	7
Presentation practice space	8	1	1	6
Performance/presentation/audience space	7	—	1	6
Classroom(s)	7	—	1	6
Food service/kitchen/catering facility	6	—	2	4
Other space	10	3	—	7

Please specify other kinds of space.

Graduate Students

"Computer cluster and soft seating area for grad students."

"Computer lab just for graduate students."

"Graduate student lockers; for group study room: collaborative group work space and 4 computer workstations."

"We have a pilot project coming up which will provide semi-enclosed study rooms for graduate student study rentable on a weekly basis. The area will have keypad entry."

Faculty

"Individual faculty study offices."

Both

"Exhibitions."

"Graduate student Teaching Assistants tend to use library space for 'office hours.' We also have carrels assigned to grad students in 3 libraries."

"Research study carrels are open to faculty and to doctoral students who have passed their comprehensive exams."

"Space for socializing will be separate lounges for faculty and graduate students in Olin design for the first phase. There will not be a kitchen but there will be a coffee machine and other amenities to support work breaks and food consumption."

"Space to work on digital projects."

"Work spaces for media specialists to assist and teach faculty and graduate students interested in 3D modeling and visualization; audio creation and production; digital video editing; high-resolution scanning; CD and DVD authoring tools; and large format printing. In addition, there are workspaces for course management specialists to assist faculty and graduate students who are teaching and making use of the course management systems, Chalk (the University's local implementation of Blackboard)."

Other

"Computers and wireless access, special non-circulating collection of classics, graduate reserves."

"Cubicles and tables for consultations."

"In addition to over 100 locked study rooms available to faculty and graduate students in The D.B. Weldon Library, there are individual seating areas and collaborative study rooms available to all users in all library locations. The Teaching Support Centre offers training spaces, presentation practice space, meeting space, and recording/videotaping room."

"In three newly renovated branches we provide individual study carrels in lockable storage cabinet for laptop, books, papers, etc. Keys are loaned to the graduate student. Developing a Graduate Student Lounge for

Faculty of Arts PhD students in the Humanities & Social Sciences. This discrete area will support 20 study carrels, comfortable seating and coffee making facilities for our Graduate students. Space extremely limited in Arts Building and many PhD students are not provided with offices. Longer term plans will see large areas in our main branch renovated with lockable cabinets attached to graduate student study carrels, targeting MA students, not UG."

"Only individual study carrels are provided to graduate students but most of the other spaces and services are available to graduate students along with other library patrons."

"Private self-contained carrels with door locks."

14. Please indicate the relative proportions of the kinds of physical environments available in the service space(s). N=29

Percentage of space for quiet study/reflection N=26

Minimum	Maximum	Mean	Median	Std Dev
10%	100%	73.08%	85%	29.61

Percentage of space for louder collaborative work N=19

Minimum	Maximum	Mean	Median	Std Dev
5%	100%	33.37%	30%	29.02

Percentage of space for presentations/performance N=8

Minimum	Maximum	Mean	Median	Std Dev
5%	100%	21.63%	10%	32.16

Percentage of space for classrooms/training/meetings N=9

Minimum	Maximum	Mean	Median	Std Dev
5%	30%	15.22%	10%	8.61

Quiet Study	Collaboration	Presentations	Classrooms	Comments
10				
20	10	10	10	The rest of the space is collections. The space for other activities will grow as more collections are moved off-site.
23	11	23	27	There is some overlap between the categories listed above. For example, two of the smaller conference rooms are used for louder collaborative work and for smaller meetings.
25	65	10		
50	30	5	15	This applies to all of our subject specific libraries.
50	40		10	
50	50			
50	50			
60	15	5	20	
67	33			
70	30			
80	5	10	5	
80	10		10	
90	10			
90	10			
90	10			
95	5			
100		100		The Roger C. Holden Faculty and Graduate Student Reading Room is typically configured for quiet study, but it is occasionally used for events and presentations. The room is either configured 100% for quiet study, or 100% for presentations/events. The Science Library Faculty and Graduate Student Reading Room is always configured for quiet study.
100				Difficult to answer this question as the Faculty Writing Place is quiet unless there is an event going on with food, speaker, and collaboration or a group comes in. It's the same space used for a variety of purposes. A classroom is adjoining and connected by a hallway.

Quiet Study	Collaboration	Presentations	Classrooms	Comments
100				
100				
100				
100				
100				
100				
100				
	60	10	30	
	90		10	
	100			Of the facilities restricted for graduate/ professional students only in the Owen Library, the group study/meeting rooms are the only service points in that category. Quiet study space, service desk, etc. are accessible to all university patrons as well as Owen students.

SERVICES PROVIDED

15. Which of the following **technology resources and services** are available for use in the service space(s)? Check all that apply. N=36

		Graduate Students	Faculty	Both
	N	10	5	24
Desktop computers	24	6	3	15
Reproduction equipment (printers, scanners, photocopiers, etc.)	21	5	3	13
Loaner laptop computers	18	3	2	13
Display surfaces (blackboards, interactive whiteboards, etc.)	18	5	3	10
Computer peripheral equipment, either on site or loans (data projectors, headsets, microphones, etc.)	15	4	1	10
General software (Word, Excel, etc.) workshops/assistance	14	3	2	9
Viewing or listening equipment	12	1	1	10
Printing/scanning services (staff-mediated)	11	2	1	8
AV equipment, either on site or loans (projectors, video recorders, etc.)	9	1	—	8
Digitization services (staff-mediated)	8	1	1	6
Other technology services	14	1	2	11

Please specify other technology services.

Graduate

"Wireless coverage."

Faculty

"Faculty are the only user group that has laptops reserved for their use. Student laptops available to both graduate and undergraduate students."

"The Retired Faculty research room includes one computer, a printer, and a fax machine."

Both

"All Individual Research Study Rooms have access to the Library's wireless network."

"All the above services are available in the library. There is no specific area set aside for graduates or faculty except study carrels."

"Facilities for conducting usability studies; facilities for experimenting with new technology and software; self-service scanning."

"GIS, data, and visualization technologies."

"Many of these services are available, but not from a faculty/grad student desk. Much of what we envision is still just that—a vision."

"Most of the above services are available to all users in those and in other spaces. Some are used more heavily by faculty, such as digital production services. Video conferencing will also be more targeted toward faculty and graduate students."

"Some digitization, staff-mediated, technology services are in the planning stages."

"Sound booth; 3D visualization space."

"Teaching Support Centre: ack computer, CD, DVD, Smart Board, Sympodium, camera and recording equipment, overhead projector. Western Libraries: desktop computers available for use by all users."

"This is a confusing question since our services are distributed. We provide many of these services in spaces not exclusively dedicated to faculty/graduate students. Additionally we provide some of these services to graduate students who are instructors (GSI), who are considered in a category of teachers, rather than just all graduate students. Also one of our subject specialty libraries loans laptops currently but primarily to their department only so I didn't mark that option."

"Working on a collaboration with our Teaching and Learning Center on incorporating technology into the classroom."

16. Which of the following **research services** are provided to graduate students and/or faculty in the service space(s)? Check all that apply. N=27

	N	Graduate Students	Faculty	Both
		4	2	24
Remote Reference/Research Help service (e-mail, chat, virtual reference, etc.)	25	3	1	21
Citation Management software and assistance	20	3	1	16
Appointment-based Reference/Research Help	18	2	1	15
Data analysis and/or software assistance	14	2	—	12
Reference/Research Help Desk service (face-to-face)	13	1	—	12
GIS analysis and/or software assistance	13	3	—	10
Organizing conferences or colloquiums	3	—	1	2
Other research services	9	—	1	8

Please specify other research services.

Faculty

"Center for Teaching; instructional design."

Both

"All except organizing conferences/colloquiums are available in the main library. No separate area for grads or faculty."

"Digital media support; support for the University's course management system."

"Graduate Student Workshop Series — already being offered but coordination will be transferred to the Chapman Learning Commons."

"Interlibrary services/document delivery."

"Many of these services are available, but not from a faculty/grad student desk. Much of what we envision is still just that—a vision."

"Media Production provides information graphics and research posters. The Library's chief collection development officer also has an office in the Faculty Commons."

"Organizing and publicizing talks by experts."

"Rush order materials requested by faculty and graduate students that are within the collecting mandate of the Libraries."

17. Which of the following **teaching support services** are provided to graduate students and/or faculty in the service space(s)? Check all that apply. N=17

	N	Graduate Students	Faculty	Both
		0	1	16
Instructional skills workshops and assistance	14	—	1	13
Educational technology workshops and assistance	13	—	—	13
Learning object creation workshops and assistance	7	—	—	7
Podcasting	7	—	—	7
Video conferencing	6	—	—	6
Vodcasting	4	—	—	4
Other teaching support services	4	—	—	4

Please specify other teaching support services.

Both

"Centre for Teaching and Academic Growth (TAG); Office of Learning Technology have offices in IKBLC. Faculty of Graduate Studies and Writing Centre and other potential partners still to be determined. See url's at end of survey responses."

"Many of the options above are provided by the campus' Educational Technology Services which is not part of the library but which we partner with on many projects, including elements of their educational technology workshop."

"Web 2.0 tools, electronic portfolios, Blackboard assistance, learning design."

"Whatever our Teaching and Learning Center will provide."

18. Which of the following **personal growth services** are provided to graduate students and/or faculty in the service space(s)? Check all that apply. N=18

	N	Graduate Students	Faculty	Both
		2	2	15
Library information literacy/bibliographic instruction sessions	15	2	—	13
Academic content development	6	—	—	6
Writing clinic/editing services	6	—	2	4
Dissertation completion support/thesis coaches	5	1	—	4
Peer tutoring/mentoring	4	—	—	4
Numeracy sessions	3	—	—	3
Academic skills counselling (time management, etc.)	3	—	—	3
ESL services/translation services	1	—	—	1
Personal counselling (anxiety, depression, etc.)	—	—	—	—
Other personal growth services	1	—	—	1

Please specify other personal growth services.

"Potentially, all may be offered (tbd)."

Additional comments about services

"Although we do provide many of the above services to graduate students and faculty, we do not limit those services to just faculty and graduate students."

"Library literacy, academic content, writing clinic, per tutoring are offered in main library. No separate area for grads or faculty."

"Many of these services are provided already by campus in other locations than the Library."

"We offer many of these services through our SMART Learning Commons which is open to all students. We have a grad student research guide available online. We offer a series of grad student workshops in the fall semester."

"Western Libraries: Library information literacy/bibliographic instruction sessions. Teaching Support Centre: all checked. Although translation is not provided, there are special services offered to international graduate students and faculty."

19. Does the library partner with any of the campus units below to deliver services for graduate students and/or faculty? If yes, please:

- briefly describe the role each partner has played;

- describe from where the partner provides services. (For example, do the campus partners maintain permanent offices or satellite offices in the library? Alternatively, do they provide services in library spaces but maintain their permanent offices elsewhere?);

- indicate whether the library has formal contracts or memorandums of understanding (MOUs) with the partner outlining rights and responsibilities associated with their use of physical space or involvement in research/teaching support services

N=44

	Partner		MOU		
	Yes	No	No	Some Arrangements	All Arrangements
Campus Computing	27	15	16	8	2
Faculty Development/ Teaching Excellence Office	18	22	17	—	—
Writing Center	15	25	13	1	—
Learning Technoligies Office	15	25	13	1	—
Office of Research	11	28	11	—	—
Graduate Student Development Office	10	30	9	—	—
Other Partner	10	28	9	—	1
Total number of respondents	31	38	24	8	3

Campus Computing N=42

Yes	27	64%
No	15	36%

No formal contracts or MOUs	16	62%
Some arrangements are documented through contracts or MOUs	8	31%
All arrangements are documented with contracts or MOUs	2	7%

Role	Provides Services from:	MOU?	Comments
Academic application support	Another building on campus	No	
Campus mainframe servers	Located in the library	No	
Columbia University IT Department	DSSC	No	CUIT supports equipment interface, server maintenance, assists in user consultations by providing technical advice.
Computer lab help desk	Computer lab in library	All	
Computing labs open to all campus community	Two libraries	Some	
Consortium of colleges provides computing support and laptops for loan; help desk; downloadable software	Most library buildings	Some	
For all users: IT help desk in library, wired and wireless network support, provide workstations and printers, security cameras for computing resources	Help desk in Library and OIT offices outside library	No	
I.T. Help Desk, Teaching lab computer support	Library and other locations	Some	MOU for use of shared, computer-equipped classrooms in library.
IT has a help desk in 3 spaces that cater to grad students and faculty.	Scholars Lab, the humanities/social sciences library, the science library, and the Institute for Advanced Technology in the Humanities which is housed in the library	Some	
IT help desk	Computer lab located in the main library	No	

Role	Provides Services from:	MOU?	Comments
IT help desk located in our Information Commons	Password reset, general technology help with laptops and approved software	No	
IT help desk, wireless network support	ITS and occasionally from within the libraries early in the academic term	No	
IT Help Desk, wireless network support, data services support	Campus computing centers and library	No	
IT help desk, wireless network support, server management	ICS, NCS, Ancillary Services	Some	ICS, Service Level Agreement, Ancillary Service Agreement
IT help desk, wireless network, hardware/software discounts	IT location	No	
Library/IT Help Desk, wireless support, computer classrooms, key served software	This building and others	No	
Productivity workstations		All	
Provides a computer lab within the library for graduate students		No	
Providing equipment and support for services,	Help desk in the Information Commons. Other services include an advanced visualization lab, humanities and social sciences digitization support, Stat-Math Lab, GIS	No	We have an MOU for the Information Commons with UITS, our central computer organization. Still in planning phases for Research Commons.
The Campus Computing's Academic Technologies group staffs this service point.		No	The Library's Integrated Library Systems Group and the Library's Digital Library Development Center staff share office space with the Computing Organization's Academic Technologies Group. The Academic Technology group's staff provides the equipment and services to faculty and graduate students from this space.

Role	Provides Services from:	MOU?	Comments
The Library provides space to campus computing, writing, and instructional learning services who support faculty and graduate students by providing wireless laptop assistance, instructional design, writing, and classroom technology support services. This exists to some extent at branch libraries as well.	Within the main library	No	This is in a pilot stage.
They are the primary force in this project, and the staff in the area will report to CIO and provide the services.	The library location	No	
Wireless network support	In library spaces but maintain their permanent offices elsewhere	No	
Wireless network support, some off-site server management, IT help desk (outside the library)-not specific to any user group	Offices outside the library	Some	
Wireless network, computing infrastructure	Permanent offices elsewhere	Some	
www.it.ubc.ca			
Yes, IT help, wireless network support and server management	On location and remotely	Some	

Additional Comments

"We don't collaborate on physical service points; but we're doing a lot with customized portal views."

"The library has an MOU with campus computing for general services, but not specifically for graduate students or faculty."

"The Libraries do provide a Statistical Software Consulting service. Again, this is not limited to faculty and graduate students."

Faculty Development/Teaching Excellence Office N=40

Yes	18	45%
No	22	55%

No formal contracts or MOUs	17	100%
Some arrangements are documented through contracts or MOUs	—	—
All arrangements are documented with contracts or MOUs	—	—

Role	Provides services from:	MOU?	Comments
Centre for Teaching and Academic Growth http://www.tag.ubc.ca	Unspecified		Librarians attend courses offered by TAG on teaching skills; librarians also deliver information literacy courses through TAG.
Coordinate teaching needs assessment, Blackboard use, electronic reserves.	Library	No	
Co-sponsor service and hold events.	Another building	No	
In discussion stages now.	To be determined	No	
Librarians offer workshops as part of new faculty orientation	Centre for Support of Teaching	No	
Pedagogical program and skill development	Teaching Support Centre in The D.B. Weldon Library	No	
Range of workshops, grants, coordination of programs	Variety of campus locations based on size of room available, some in library	No	Campus does not formally have a teaching excellence center, rather a collaborative group of campus partners supporting faculty/ instructor development including the library.
Research, teaching, and leadership development of faculty and graduates including workshops, seminars, consultations, etc.	Center for Faculty Excellence located in the main library	No	
Space for faculty development workshops	Offices and space in Library	No	

Role	Provides services from:	MOU?	Comments
The Center for Teaching and Learning offers workshops, discussion series, individual consultations, and other programming and resources to develop and strengthen teaching skills and strategies.	Offices within Faculty Commons	No	
The library provides sessions in the August and January teaching workshops.	The Teaching Resource Center	No	
These are already in the building, Teaching and Learning Technology Center	Their existing space in Library West Tower.	No	Predates our development of an MOU process.
Workshops	Classroom	No	
Workshops	Permanent offices elsewhere	No	
Workshops are offered to faculty concerning copyright issues, using bibliographic management software, and linking to library services in course management pages.	These workshops are held at the Institute for Teaching and Learning Excellence facility on campus.	No	Workshops for using bibliographics management software are also held in the library training room, but these classes are also open to undergraduate students.
Workshops on library resources	Library classrooms	No	
Unspecified	Unspecified	No	Some collaboration with the Sheridan Teaching Center but not formal
Unspecified	Teaching & Learning Services	No	

Writing Center N=40

Yes	15	37%
No	25	63%

No formal contracts or MOUs	13	93%
Some arrangements are documented through contracts or MOUs	1	7%
All arrangements are documented with contracts or MOUs	—	—

Role	Provides services from:	MOU?	Comments:
All kinds of writing tutoring for whole campus population - drop-in and scheduled 45 minute sessions; workshops	Our building	No	
Coordinated support for writing intensive classes	Library	No	
Dissertation assistance, writing, tutoring, editing dissertations as well as organizing them.	Service point in combination with other services targeted for Undergrads.	No	Not at this point, but there will be an MOU.
English Center provides writing tutoring to ENGL core writing courses	Liberal Arts classroom building and Library satellite location in carrels	No	
Joint consultation services and workshops	Main library	No	
Potential			
Provide faculty development and institutional services that support a writing-centered curriculum; offer faculty workshops and individual consultations in teaching development.	Offices within Faculty Commons	No	Student writing center is located in the Learning Commons.
Range of support for student services (though mainly undergraduate)	Usually their department, though had a trial satellite in library (cancelled due to their budget/ staff cuts)	Some	
Referral, some joint teaching	Main library	No	
The Writing Center is moving to the main library. They serve all students.		No	

Role	Provides services from:	MOU?	Comments:
The Writing Center is part of SMART Commons, but not limited to grad students.		No	
Tutor; not specific to any user group	Classroom	No	
We have a pilot project starting in May where the writing centre will have a presence on the main floor of Scott Library in preparation for the upcoming Learning Commons initiative.	Main floor and will also use library teaching spaces to conduct workshops.	No	
Writing Center is located in building	Discussing having writing assistants at our general reference desk.	No	
Writing clinic	Within the library satellite office	No	

Additional Comments

"The Writing Center does maintain library office hours, but the service is open to all. There is also no formal contract for this activity."

"We have a partnership with the writing center, but it is primarily geared toward undergraduate students, not graduates."

"Writing Center has a service point in Main Library, but no services specifically targeted at grad students (or faculty)."

Learning Technologies Office N=39

Yes	15	39%
No	24	61%

No formal contracts or MOUs	13	93%
Some arrangements are documented through contracts or MOUs	1	6%
All arrangements are documented with contracts or MOUs.	—	—

Role	Provides services from:	MOU?	Comments
Assisted technology equipment	Friedman Study Center for both Under Grads and Grads - all hours open (24 x 5)	No	
Collaborative workshops	Permanent offices elsewhere	No	
Content & Collaboration Services		No	
Coordinate teaching needs assessment, Blackboard use, electronic reserves	Shared teaching lab in library	No	
Faculty and graduate e-learning support, learning management system support, learning object creations, etc.	Center for Faculty Excellence located in the main library	No	
Instructional design classes and consultations. Focus on technologies to enhance creative teaching	Five staff have offices in the library.	No	
Learning design	Offices within Faculty Commons	No	
Learning management systems assistance	Educational technology lab, and library	No	
Learning management systems workshops, Learning Object Creation, Multimedia support, Videoconferencing support	Library and other locations	Some	Shared classrooms have an MOU.

Role	Provides services from:	MOU?	Comments
Learning management systems, webcasting/podcasting courses	Main building with technology infrastructure for this department, distributed to many classrooms	No	Many of the collaborative elements with this group are focused on meetings for designing services such as those integrated in the learning management system, so those meetings might take place in the library or elsewhere.
Office of Learning Technology			
Oncourse (CMS) support	Teaching and Learning Technology Center.	No	The existence of this service point pre-dates our development of MOUs.
Partner with both the Teaching Support Centre and Western Libraries to provide learning technologies and program skill development	Teaching Support Centre in The D. B. Weldon Library	No	
Workshops on systems and software; help developing online courseroom standards	Their location	No	
Workshops, technology fair	Classrooms, large meeting space	No	

Office of Research N=39

Yes	11	28%
No	28	72%

No formal contracts or MOUs	10	100%
Some arrangements are documented through contracts or MOUs	—	—
All arrangements are documented with contracts or MOUs	—	—

Role	Provides services from:	MOU?	Comments:
Copyright advice and assistance	Library	No	
Development and support for electronic theses and dissertations and teaching about avoiding plagiarism	Various locations	No	
Digital repository cooperation	Another building	No	
Grant processing.		No	
Grant workshops, NIH and copyright workshops, NIH submissions	Permanent offices elsewhere	No	
IP advice		No	
Main focus has been on open access/ scholarly communication lately	Distributed	No	
Submits library grants to grantors on behalf of university; partners with library on intellectual property	Their office location; online-- mostly staff e-mail	No	
Supporting the Arts and Humanities Institute to be located in the RC,	Remodeled space on the first floor.	No	
We offer grants workshops that are attended primarily by faculty and grad students.		No	

Graduate Student Development Office N=40

Yes	10	25%
No	30	75%

No formal contracts or MOUs	9	100%
Some arrangements are documented through contracts or MOUs	—	—
All arrangements are documented with contracts or MOUs	—	—

Role	Provides Services from:	MOU?	Comments:
Demonstrating various thesis and dissertations that have been done electronically rather than in print. Explaining the time lapse between completion of thesis/dissertation and appearance in library catalog and in digital dissertations database.	Various college classrooms.	No	
Electronic theses and dissertations workshops taught in library classrooms	Library and other locations	No	
Graduate student professional development programs	Graduate College, and library	No	
Many workshops, partner with major grant for instructor development	Generally in meeting spaces across campus	No	
Publishing workshops, alert service workshops	Permanent offices elsewhere	No	
Research grant and dissertation writing clinics and other joint workshops	Main library	No	
Support for the development of services for grad students; advising; theses and dissertation help, career support	Currently, they provide services in another building. They also support the Grad Grants center in the Wells Library.	No	This service predates our MOU process.
We offer library orientation for graduate students at the program level		No	
Unspecified	Unspecified	No	

Other Partner 1 N=10

No formal contracts or MOUs	9	90%
Some arrangements are documented through contracts or MOUs	—	—
All arrangements are documented with contracts or MOUs	1	10%

Name and Role:	Provides Services from:	MOU?	Comments:
Study Partners tutoring service; Honors College; Encyclopedia of Alabama Digital Project, Graduate student council, campus food services	Dedicated space in Library; Offices in Library; First two have office space; food service runs a coffee shop and coffee kiosk.	No	
Intercollegiate Athletics; Campus collaborations for developing common online systems and instructional technology	Central office; Committees that include membership from library	No	
Provost	See comments	All	VIVO—virtual academic community
Art Department	Student art exhibit space created in the Library	No	
Informatics Program	Virtual program	No	
Academic Advising and international programs assistance with majors, course selection, degree completion requirement, internships; Learning Resource Center: academic tutoring and supplemental instruction; Career Services: resume writing, career selection, internships	Our Learning Commons and their building; Our building; Our building and another	No	
Office of Campus-Community Engagement	Offices within Faculty Commons	No	This Campus-Community Engagement staff serve as consultants who help faculty and administrators develop partnerships with local and regional agencies.
Workshops in the Fall on using library services and facilities for international graduate students.	Library training room	No	Director of Library Graduate and Research Services invites international graduate students to attend the workshops at the university international student orientation sessions.

Name and Role:	Provides Services from:	MOU?	Comments:
Services for Students with Disabilities, a unit within Student Development Services — support to students with disabilities, including graduate students	Space provided in The D.B. Weldon Library	No	
Statistical Analysis Unit — Main Library	Provide assistance in gathering and analyzing research statistics	No	

SERVICE POINT STAFFING

If there is one or more service point specifically designated for delivering graduate student and/or faculty services, please answer the following staffing questions. Otherwise, continue to the next page.

20. For each category of staff below please indicate how many individuals provide services to graduate students and/or faculty (enter a whole number, e.g., 4) and the FTE of these individuals (enter a whole number or a two-digit decimal, e.g., 3.25). N=10

Librarian N=6

Individuals	FTE
1	0.5
1	1
1	1
3	3
25	—
—	6

Other library professional N=5

Individuals	FTE
1	1
2	2
2	—
1	—
—	1

Library support staff N=4

Individuals	FTE
5	5
4	4
5	—
1	—

Student assistants N=4

Individuals	FTE
6	2
7	2.25
10	—
—	3

Campus computing staff N=3

Individuals	FTE
2	—
6	6
—	4

Faculty development office staff N=2

Individuals	FTE
2	2
9	—

Writing center staff N=2

Individuals	FTE
3	3
3	—

Learning technologies office staff N=3

Individuals	FTE
7	4
3	—
5	—

Student development office staff N=1

Individuals	FTE
1	—

Graduate studies department staff N=1

Individuals	FTE
2	—

Other staff category N=1

Individuals	FTE
1	1

Other partner staff N=1

Individuals	FTE
2	2

Office of research staff N=0

Respondent	Librarian	Other library professional	Library support staff	Student assistants	Campus computing staff	Faculty development office staff	Learning technologies office staff	Student development office staff	Graduate studies department staff	Writing center staff	Other partner staff	Other staff category
1	1	1		6								
2	1	2		7		2	7			3	2	1
3	1		5									
4	3		4									
5	25		5	10	2	9	3	1	2	3		
6					6							
7	6 FTE	2	1	3 FTE	4							
8							5					
9		1										
10		1 FTE										

21. Is there a director/coordinator position specifically assigned to overseeing spaces or services for graduate students and/or faculty? N=26

Yes	9	35%
No	17	65%

If yes, please enter the position title and the title of the position to which it reports. N=9

Position title:	Reports to:
Associate Director, Client Services, Sciences, Health & Engineering	Director of Libraries
Co-director-Center for Digital Research in the Humanities	Dean of Libraries
Director of Public Services	Associate University Librarian for Collections and Services
Director of System Wide Public Services	Deputy University Librarian
Director, NSIT Academic Technologies, Instructional Technology & Design	Senior Director, NSIT Academic Technologies
Director, Virginia Campus Library	Associate University Librarian
DSpace Product Manager	Associate Director for Public Services
Head of Graduate Services	Humanities Librarian
Head, Access Services & Collections	Director, Biomedical Library

22. How were staff positions for graduate student and/or faculty spaces and services created? Check all that apply. N=14

Library redefined job descriptions of existing staff	7	50%
Library created new positions	6	43%
Library reassigned staff to new service point	5	36%
Partners reassigned staff to new service point	5	36%
Partners created new positions	3	21%
Partners redefined job descriptions of existing staff	3	21%
Library staff applied to work in the new service point	—	—
Partners staff applied to work in the new service point	—	—
Other	3	21%

Respondent	Library			Partner		
	Created	Redefined	Reassigned	Created	Redefined	Reassigned
1	✔	✔	✔	✔	✔	✔
2	✔	✔	✔	✔		
3	✔	✔				
4	✔	✔				
5		✔	✔		✔	✔
6		✔	✔			✔
7		✔				
8	✔			✔		
9	✔					
10			✔			✔
11					✔	✔

Please explain other.

"Library has had this service point for so long it has been an assumed role."

"Unable to give breakdown of staff. Re staff positions created: the alignment of the Libraries strategic plan with University strategic directions influenced the rebalancing of existing unit workloads to incorporate an emphasis on research and graduate education."

"We are still in the planning stages for the Research Commons so don't have specifics for staffing, but do know that there will be staffing from units outside the libraries and that the library will redefine or expand responsibilities for existing staff."

23. How are your graduate student and/or faculty services and spaces marketed to the campus community? Check all that apply. N=41

Word of mouth	38	93%
Principal library Web site	28	68%
Printed literature (brochures, bookmarks, etc.)	28	68%
Tours/orientation	28	68%
Visits to faculty and departmental meetings	24	59%
E-mail announcements targeting graduate students	21	51%
Visits to graduate student meetings	17	42%
E-mail announcements targeting faculty members	16	39%
Posters	7	17%
Separate research commons Web site	3	7%
Other strategies	8	20%

Please describe other strategies.

"Coordination with Graduate Division newsletter/coordinator."

"General library publicity about new services."

"Office hours in departmental offices."

"Plasma screens in Faculty Commons and on other floors in library. Library's subject specialists have been enlisted to spread the word."

"Press releases; campus calendars"

"Public computer screen savers and plasma screens, Facebook ads (for graduate students), campus publications."

"Spaces identified in building layouts and signage on the doors."

"We market the Faculty and Graduate reading room with a fall reception for new grad students."

24. Is there a formal marketing plan for reaching graduate students and/or faculty? N=41

Yes	8	20%
No	33	80%

Comments

Yes

"But at this point mostly for faculty and for grad students who are working as TAs."

"Faculty and graduate students are reached by visits to academic departments, new faculty orientation, new graduate student orientation, and library publications geared to all users."

"The library's marketing plan includes graduate students as a market segment."

"We are developing an orientation publication for new graduate students and we have a campus-wide graduate student orientation event in the library. The event is part of the formal orientation program for graduate students co-sponsored by the Graduate School and the Graduate and Professional Students Association."

"We produce online newsletters for faculty that go out twice a year."

No

"Marketing to graduate students and faculty is included in an overall marketing strategy for the Libraries. However, specific resources and services for faculty and graduate students are promoted through the Western Libraries Web site, through subject librarians who have built relationships with faculty and graduate student groups, and through individual marketing campaigns in each of the libraries. The new Web site design expected to be ready for fall 2008 has incorporated information gathered from faculty and graduate students for a site that better meets their needs, including the promotion of resources and services."

"There are very limited faculty study spaces and graduate student carrels; therefore we purposefully depend only on word of mouth and do not market their availability. There is always a waiting list for these spaces."

"We are currently developing a marketing plan for the library system and marketing services/spaces to graduate students. Faculty will be included in that plan."

"We will work with the Marketing Librarian on this initiative, but a plan has not yet been created."

25. What statistics are kept to track graduate student and/or faculty use of spaces and services? Check all that apply. N=44

No usage statistics kept	14	32%
Sessions (# of sessions, type of sessions, # of participants in average session, and total served for a particular function)	12	27%
Head counts by time or location	9	21%
Gate counts/exit counts	8	18%
Questions answered	7	16%
By department served (departmental affiliation)	7	16%
Web or print comments	7	16%
Web usage (page hits, etc.)	6	14%
By specific courses supported	6	14%
Other	17	39%

Please specify other.

"Actual number of requests for graduate student document delivery."

"Carrel applications by department and rank."

"Circulation data for specific populations."

"Circulation statistics for graduate students; consultations with selected graduate students; ILLO stats are another possible option we haven't explored."

"Document Delivery support; statements in dissertations."

"Grants received."

"Included with overall statistics."

"Information not available yet."

"Keep track of access cards issued to grad students to use the Group Study Room. Track the number of lockers checked out/in use each year."

"Occasional task forces and special projects usually indicating respondents classification (i.e., graduate student, faculty, etc.)"

"Occupancy is always at 100%; we monitor the queue line for the waiting lists."

"Reference questions and instructional efforts are tracked."

"Statistics are maintained on the number of Faculty Research Studies assigned per semester and the number of graduate research carrels assigned."

"Statistics regarding room assignments."

"The number of carrels assigned to faculty and grad students is tracked."

"We are in the process of doing focus groups with graduate students about the plans for the Research Commons."

"We keep statistics on these things but they are not segregated by user status.'

26. **How is satisfaction with spaces and services for graduate students and/or faculty assessed? Check all that apply. N=41**

No formal assessment	6	15%
LibQUAL+®	26	63%
Suggestion boxes/boards	18	44%
In-house surveys	17	42%
Focus groups	15	37%
Interviews	8	20%
Broad-based research studies	1	2%
Other	10	24%

Please specify other.

"Academic support unit program reviews."

"Anecdotal data."

"In house surveys and triennial surveys sent to all faculty/staff/students."

"Information not available yet."

"In-house surveys and focus groups and other assessment plans/programs – tbd."

"LibQUAL+® was done in 2006; other assessments are on-going."

"Surveys run by Graduate Student Organization."

"This is not limited to graduate students and faculty. We also have a liaison librarian who works with each department as their personal librarian for service and collection issues."

"Voluntary comments on Web page."

"We are now doing our own assessment."

ADDITIONAL COMMENTS

27. Please enter any additional information about spaces or services specifically designed for graduate students and/or faculty that may assist the authors in accurately analyzing the results of this survey. N=25

Selected Comments from Respondents

"1. The collection at the branch campus library is specifically geared to the graduate and faculty classes and research. 2. Plans for a grant writing center to support this activity. 3. The main library offers closed study rooms (small offices) for doctoral candidates."

"A large portion of this survey does not pertain to us because while we do provide, and have always provided, separate study spaces for faculty and graduate students, we do not provide any separate services or service points for these groups."

"A position was created to provide and coordinate more services of interest to faculty and graduate students, but as of yet no space or services have been limited to just these user groups. Discussions have been held after interview sessions and focus groups with graduate students concerning more services and spaces for graduate students. Among the top requests from the graduate students, and one of the most viable, has been for lockers to store books. A service that was initiated with graduate students and faculty in mind was a document delivery service. Previously graduate students and faculty could only request (ILL) items not owned by the library. Last year the new document delivery service was begun. If the library owns the journal that contains an article a student or faculty member wants, they can request it and the library will pull the journal from the shelf and make an electronic copy of the article for the student much in the same way we fulfill Interlibrary Loan Requests. The same rules of ILL apply to make sure fair use is maintained. If the library owns a book the student or faculty member would like, they can request it and the library will pull the book and hold it at the circulation desk for them."

"At this point in time, our library does not have particular services focused for grad students and faculty. We do have a graduate library 4 miles east of the main campus, that serves a few specific graduate programs, located on that campus. All of the services of that branch library are primarily aimed at the grad students and faculty who make up their primary clientele. The services are the usual: reference, instruction, and circulation."

"Graduate student spaces and services are in the planning stage."

"In addition to the new service of document delivery to graduate students, the library has provided two other faculty-only services for many years. 1. Document delivery: this is very popular and appreciated. 2. Research offices, scheduled by semester, inside the library."

"In addition, there is a wing in the library that is composed of 220 faculty studies, offices that faculty can rent by the academic quarter for a small fee. These are heavily used as quiet office space for doing library research."

"Many of the responses to questions relate to plans for a renovation that has not yet taken place, however many of the services and collaborations mentioned are already in place."

"Our main library is functioning at more than 50% over capacity, so the amount of targeted spaces that we can offer to faculty and graduate students is currently limited. We try to offer a rich set of location-independent services from our Web site. We are currently in the early stages of design for a new library building, in which we will incorporate more dedicated faculty and graduate students spaces and (if needed) services."

"Ours is a huge research library at a giant university. We have nine primarily library buildings, almost all of which offer collections and services targeted to graduate students and faculty. There are also departmental libraries and reading rooms that are not under the library's management, and these do a substantial amount of focus on graduate students and faculty that would otherwise be done by the university library system and staff if these libraries were reporting to us. Some of them have librarians; some do not. We don't always know about their activities, promotions, or marketing. This made some of the survey questions a bit difficult to answer."

"The Graduate Study Room just opened this semester and we are just beginning to look at making it fully operational. We will be introducing more services and opportunities for graduate students in the future."

"The library is interested in and is studying new ways of providing new types of collaborative flexible spaces for faculty and graduate students that go beyond existing services."

"This is a new facility and still very much in a developmental phase. Although we have used participant surveys to assess individual events (workshops, etc.) held in the Faculty Commons, we have not used LibQUAL+®, focus groups, or formal interviews since the opening of this facility, but we have plans to do so."

"We are designing both a teaching commons (to be opening summer or fall) and a research commons. These will completely change our responses to these questions."

"We are just in the research and discussion stages of this project and have not gotten far enough along to make much of a contribution to this survey. We will be interested in the results."

"We have a unique building that is divided into two towers. The smaller of the two, the West Tower, has been remodeled into an Information Commons with five floors of services and space designed for undergraduates. To complement that and to recognize the need for services designed for graduate students and faculty we are looking at the East Tower as the Research Commons, including the extensive collections in the humanities and social sciences. Creation of the Research Commons in the library will offer support—in one central campus location—to faculty and graduate students at any point in the complex research process. By assembling groups and expertise now distributed throughout the campus, the Research Commons will blend technology with traditional resources to serve as a center for a wide range of scholarly activities."

"We have no special area set aside for graduates or faculty. We do have assigned carrels scattered around the library. In the partnerships section - we have informal partnerships with several departments/offices and offer services to grad students and faculty BUT not in a special space reserved for them in the library."

"We have one space and one service clearly designated for graduate students. The Graduate Study Room provides a 24/7 graduate study for medical, pharmacy students and all graduate students at the university. The lockers are assigned on a first come, first serve basis to any graduate student needing to use arts materials. They are assigned for the academic session and are renewable. They are available all hours the building in which the Arts Library is located is open."

"We have tried not to restrict access to any of our spaces or services (such as the Scholars' Lab or the McGregor Reading Room), even though they may be targeted to grad students and faculty. Exceptions are graduate carrels, a few faculty offices, and our on-Grounds deliveries for faculty. We are thinking of including graduate research space in the coming renovations of our main library, but are leaning toward more flexible, unrestricted space."

"We provide individual lockable study spaces for 16 students for a term. No other services are provided at this time."

"While I understand what you are seeking to learn, the concept does not fit well with our physical facility at this time; our spaces are more antiquated and we wouldn't currently create this sort of service at this time; in a future renovated space spaces targeted to grads and faculty makes good sense."

"While we may design and operate certain spaces with faculty and/or graduate students in mind and they will be the dominate users, in most cases other than the designated lounges planned for Olin, the Graduate study area in Mann, and the graduate carrels and faculty studies in Kroch, our spaces are open to all who need to use the space for its designated purpose. The services that we offer including research help do not differentiate between patron groups, but are available to users of those spaces. We intentionally left section 11 blank because it is impossible for us to supply such granular information across three large diverse libraries."

RESPONDING INSTITUTIONS

University at Albany, SUNY

Auburn University

Brigham Young University

University of British Columbia

Brown University

University at Buffalo, SUNY

University of California, Berkeley

University of California, Davis

University of California, Irvine

University of California, Los Angeles

University of California, San Diego

Canada Institute for Scientific and Technical Information

Case Western Reserve University

University of Chicago

University of Colorado at Boulder

Colorado State University

Columbia University

University of Connecticut

Cornell University

University of Delaware

University of Florida

George Washington University

Georgetown University

University of Georgia

University of Hawai'i at Manoa

University of Illinois at Urbana-Champaign

Indiana University Bloomington

University of Iowa

Iowa State University

Kent State University

University of Kentucky

Library of Congress

Louisiana State University

University of Louisville

McGill University

University of Manitoba

University of Massachusetts, Amherst

Massachusetts Institute of Technology

University of Minnesota

University of Nebraska–Lincoln

University of New Mexico

University of North Carolina at Chapel Hill

North Carolina State University

Ohio University

University of Oklahoma

Oklahoma State University

Pennsylvania State University

Purdue University

Rice University

Rutgers University

Smithsonian Institution

University of Southern California

Southern Illinois University Carbondale

Temple University

University of Texas at Austin

Vanderbilt University

University of Virginia

Virginia Tech

University of Washington

Washington State University

Washington University in St. Louis

University of Western Ontario

University of Wisconsin–Madison

Yale University

York University

REPRESENTATIVE DOCUMENTS

Descriptions of Services

Library A-Z | MyJosiah | Off-Campus Access | FAQ | Hours & Locations | Contact

Brown University Library

SEARCH: ⦿ Josiah ◯ WorldCat ◯ Articles ◯ Videos/DVDs   Go

QUICK LINKS
Josiah (Catalog)
WorldCat / *easyBorrow*
Course Reserves (OCRA)
Ask a Librarian
Tips & Tutorials
RefWorks
LibX

RESEARCH
Getting Started
Books, Articles, Newspapers +
Videos / DVDs
Resources by Course
Resources by Subject
Research Assistance
Copyright & Fair Use
Manage Citations

LIBRARY SERVICES
Borrow / Renew
Borrowing Options
Copying & Printing
Online Forms
Center for Digital Initiatives
Collections / A-Z
Librarians by Subject
About the Libraries

Thesis and Dissertation Binding - Information for Graduate Students

Masters and Doctoral students who wish to have personal copies of their theses/dissertations bound may deliver copies of the thesis to the Preservation Department via campus mail, via U.S. mail or in person during business hours. Our address is:

Thesis Binding
Rockefeller Library--Preservation Department
10 Prospect St. Box A
Providence, RI 02912

All theses and dissertations must be accompanied by a Binding Request Form:

- Binding Request Form (Word, PDF)
- Sample Binding Request Form (PDF)

Academic departments paying for the binding of theses, dissertations, or other materials should consult Academic Department Binding information.

Binding Style

Theses and dissertations are bound in black library cloth with gold lettering. The spine of the binding includes the title of the thesis/dissertation, the student's last name and year of completion. Special characters, such as Greek letters or mathematical symbols, may not be available for spine printing.

Payment

The charge for thesis binding is $20 per copy. Payment via credit card (Mastercard, Visa, American Express or Discover Card), Declining Balance Account or personal check is due at the time the bound items are picked up at the Gateway Services desk in the Rockefeller Library. Additional charges may apply to unusually large publications, or those with accompanying media.

- Binding Invoice
- Sample Binding Invoice

Processing Time

We ship materials to our commercial binding vendor every Tuesday. The deadline to get your thesis into the current week's shipment is 10 a.m. Monday. Theses and dissertations received after 10 a.m. on Monday may not go out until the following week's shipment. Bound items are due back two weeks after the shipment date (the day the items are sent to the vendor, not the day they are received at the library), and will be available the following day. We will notify you via email or local phone call when the bound items are ready for pick-up at the Gateway Services desk.

Special Needs

If you have binding style or processing time requirements that are unmet by the services outlined above, please contact Acme Bookbinding or another commercial binder directly to discuss your project.

The University of Chicago
L I B R A R Y

Search the Library catalog for   in
                        Keyword anywhere   Go

Catalogs   Database Finder   Hours   My Accounts   Libraries   Help

Library Home > Dissertation Office

The University of Chicago Dissertation Office

University-Wide
Requirements for the Ph.D.
Dissertation (**pdf**)

- Introduction
- Deadlines
- Requirements
- Submission Procedures
- Format
- Additional Details
  - abstract
  - copyright permissions
  - copyright registration
  - forms
  - sample title page

Quick Links

The Chicago Manual of Style Online
Encyclopædia Britannica Online
Oxford Reference Online
ProQuest Dissertation Express
ProQuest Dissertations & Theses
ProQuest Dissertations & Theses @ University of Chicago
UMI Dissertation Publishing

Forms and Additional Material

- Dissertation Packet
- Departmental Approval Form
- Publishing Your Graduate Work with UMI Dissertation Publishing
- Library Form
- Survey of Earned Doctorates

Visit the Dissertation Office

The University of Chicago Dissertation Office is located in Room 100-B of the Joseph Regenstein Library. Directions to the University of Chicago, parking information, and transportation options are noted on the UChicagoMaps site. The Library provides information about the Joseph Regenstein Library.

Regular office hours are Mondays-Thursdays, 9am-noon/1:30-4:30pm, and Fridays, 10:30am-noon/1:30-4:30pm. Actual hours may vary.

Contact the Dissertation Office

Please let us know how we can help! | Email: phd (at) lib.uchicago.edu | Phone: 773-702-7404 | Address: 1100 E. 57th St. Chicago IL 60637

Access to University of Chicago Dissertations

Where are the dissertations? U. of C. dissertations are shelved in different places and may be available online, too.

Can I buy a dissertation? Use Dissertation Express to purchase a U. of C. dissertation.

Can I borrow a dissertation? Check out a U. of C. dissertation with your Chicago Card or contact your own library for local options.

Can I search databases for dissertations? Find records for U. of C. dissertations in the library catalog, in ProQuest Dissertations & Theses @ University of Chicago, and in other databases.

May I have permission to use material from U. of C. dissertations? If your use is considered fair use according to U.S. copyright law, you do not need permission. Otherwise, you must obtain written permission from the copyright holder.

Suggestions   University Home Page   University Library Home Page   Questions and comments about this page?

The University of Chicago
L I B R A R Y

Search | the Library catalog ⬍ | for   in | Keyword anywhere ⬍ | (Go)

Catalogs · Database Finder · Hours · My Accounts · Libraries · Help

The University of Chicago Library | Information and Services for Faculty

Information and Services for Faculty

Teaching Support

Placing Course Materials on Reserve
Linking to Library Materials in Chalk
Schedule a Library Session for Your Class
Library Instruction and Curriculum Support
Request that an Item be Purchased for the Library
How the Library Can Support Academic Honesty

Research Support

Subject Bibliographers
Research Consultations

Library Access & Borrowing

Proxy Borrowers
Faculty Loan Periods & Borrowing Privileges
Using Special Collections Research Center
Library Privileges at other institutions
Library Privileges for Faculty Partners & Family
Interlibrary Loans

Library Facilities

Faculty Studies: Crerar · Regenstein
Seminar Rooms: Crerar · D'Angelo · Harper · Regenstein · Special Collections

Electronic Resources

Your Online Library Account
Accessing electronic resources from outside the Library
Wireless Internet

ID & Privileges Office Services

Class Rosters
CNet ID Assistance
Chicago Cards
CTA Tickets | Passport Photos | ITIC Cards | more...

Suggestions · University Home Page · University Library Home Page · Questions and comments about this page?

The University of Chicago Library
1100 East 57th Street Chicago Illinois 60637
Phone Numbers

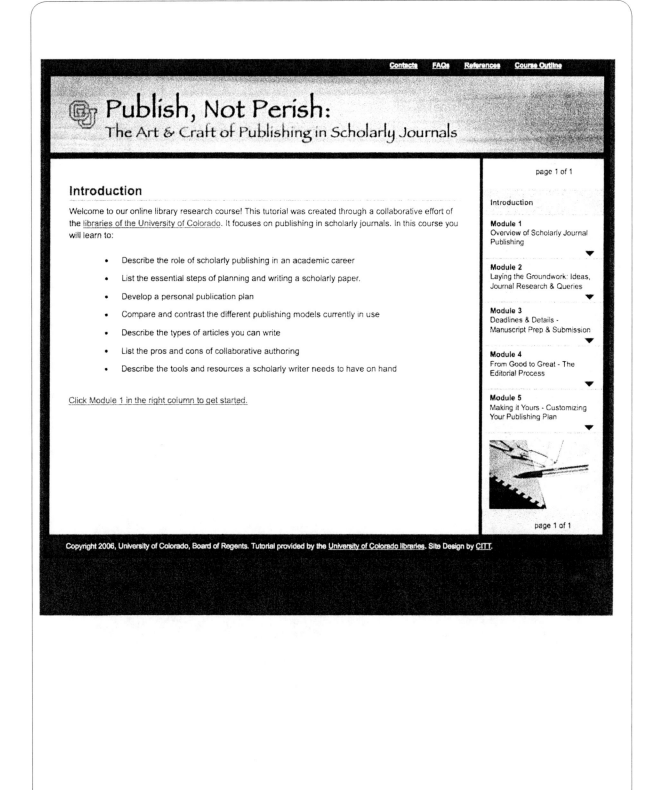

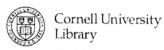

Cornell University
Library

Search Library Pages   Search Cornell

GATEWAY

| Library Catalog | Find it! Articles Databases e-Journals Images | MyLibrary | Ask a Librarian
| Individual Libraries

Faculty Office Delivery

Library **hours**

Research Tools

Instruction

Technical Support

Services

Inside CU Library

Help

ASK A LIBRARIAN
email | chat | phone

Cornell University Library

What Is It?

This service allows Faculty members to request library books for delivery to their department mail room or administrative office, Monday through Friday, during regular office hours. Requests may be placed through the Library catalog and turnaround time is expected to be 48 hours. Requests are limited to book materials from the regular circulating collection of the Ithaca and Geneva libraries; journals, videos, or other special collection items are excluded. There is no charge for this service.

How Does It Work?

Requests are placed through the "Requests" button of the library catalog (see instructions below). The library designated as your service provider (usually the library closest to your building) will check out the book to you through the library's circulation system and will deliver it to your department's mail room or administrative office within 48 hours, Monday through Friday during standard office hours. The book will arrive wrapped and labeled with your name, and will be placed in your mailbox (or in the area designated by your department coordinator). You will be notified when the book is available for you to pick up at your department.

To return books, please bring them back to any library, as you do with other library books. At this time, there is no book retrieval component to the service and the campus mail does not accept library books.

Instructions for placing a request:

- Go to the library catalog at http://catalog.library.cornell.edu.
- Locate the item you would like to request and click the "Requests" button at the top of the screen.
- Log in with your ID number and last name.
- From the Type of Request pull-down menu, select "Book Delivery."
- From the Pick Up At menu, select "Faculty Office Delivery"
- Enter your department and building address in the Comments box at the end of the screen. Submit form.
- You will be notified when the book has been delivered, or if the book cannot be delivered for any reason.

Ask a librarian | Report a problem connecting | Send us feedback | Contact Us | CU Info | CU Homepage

Library Services > Faculty > Gelman Library System Guide for GW Faculty

Faculty Recognition

Collecting Faculty Publications

The Gelman Library endeavors to collect books authored by George Washington University faculty. We purchase one copy for the GW Faculty Collection in Special Collections as well as one for our circulating collection. There is no centralized way to identify these publications so faculty are encouraged to contact the Collection Development Librarian for their department to initiate this purchase. These titles can be retrieved in our ALADIN Catalog by searching Faculty Collection as an Author.

Faculty Author Signing Events

Faculty Authors Signing Receptions are held throughout the academic year to provide an opportunity for Gelman librarians to recognize new books written by faculty authors. During the reception faculty members discuss their research, challenges they encountered, and their book's scholarly contribution within their area of study. Signed copies of the honored books are housed in the Special Collections Department's George Washington University Faculty Collection.

Emeriti Faculty

Faculty emeriti are entitled to entrance and borrowing privileges at the Gelman Library. A validated GW ID issued from the Personnel Office is necessary for borrowing items from the GW general circulating collection. Borrowing privileges are the same as those of current faculty members.

Scholarly Publication

Changes in publication and access to the record of research are sweeping through the higher education and research community. Spurred by the continuing rising costs for libraries to purchase scholarly output - prices of scientific, technical and medical journals, particularly, have risen dramatically over the last 25 years - and by advances in technology that can support new ways of reporting research, scholars are discussing the communication of their work and employing new media for dissemination of that work. See the Gelman Library System's web site on Scholarly Communication for information on new scholarly publishing initiatives, for links to related resources, and for suggestions on how to help regain control of scholarly publishing so it meets the needs of faculty and other researchers.

Return to **Gelman Guide for GW Faculty**

THE GEORGE
WASHINGTON
UNIVERSITY
WASHINGTON DC

Last modified: Wednesday, October 10, 2007 14:39:34 PM

Reference > Cybercheating

A Cybercheating Detection and Prevention Primer for GW Faculty

Created by Gelman Library, The George Washington University

Plagiarism in college is not a new phenomenon. However, with the introduction of the Internet as a research resource, the ways that students can commit plagiarism have taken on new dimensions. Online term paper mills and web sites provide students with ample opportunities to acquire materials not of their own original thought to be turned in to their classes.

Some college students today have little or no idea what constitutes plagiarism. Many of them may concede that appropriating direct quotes or paraphrasing entire pages from printed resources into their papers without proper attribution is plagiarism, but these same students would be unlikely to concede the same allowances for online material. To them, the World Wide Web is entirely free for the taking and does not require any kind of citation of sources.

The Internet has forced university faculty members to redouble their efforts to determine if students have plagiarized the papers they turn in and to continue to find ways to prevent students from plagiarizing in the first place.

Gelman Library has created this cybercheating detection & prevention primer as a way to assist GW faculty in detecting student cybercheating or online plagiarism as well as preventing it. It is aimed at providing you with the background education and access to resources needed to conduct your own independent investigation of potential cybercheating.

Table of Contents

This web site is maintained by Tina Plottel.

THE GEORGE
WASHINGTON
UNIVERSITY
WASHINGTON DC

Last modified: Wednesday, 03-Jan-2007 14:51:01 EST

UNIVERSITY OF MINNESOTA: Copyright Information & Education

http://www.lib.umn.edu/copyright/

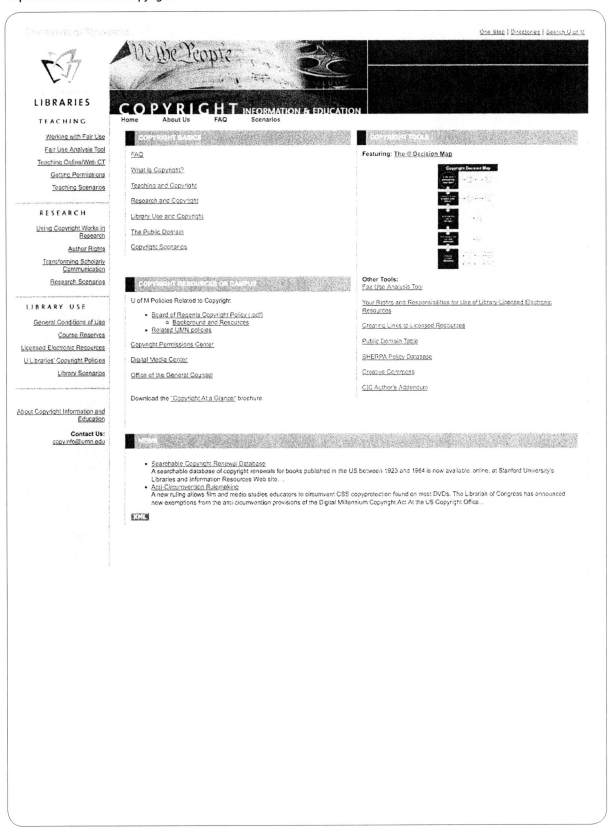

http://www.libraries.rutgers.edu/rul/lib_servs/faculty_services.shtml

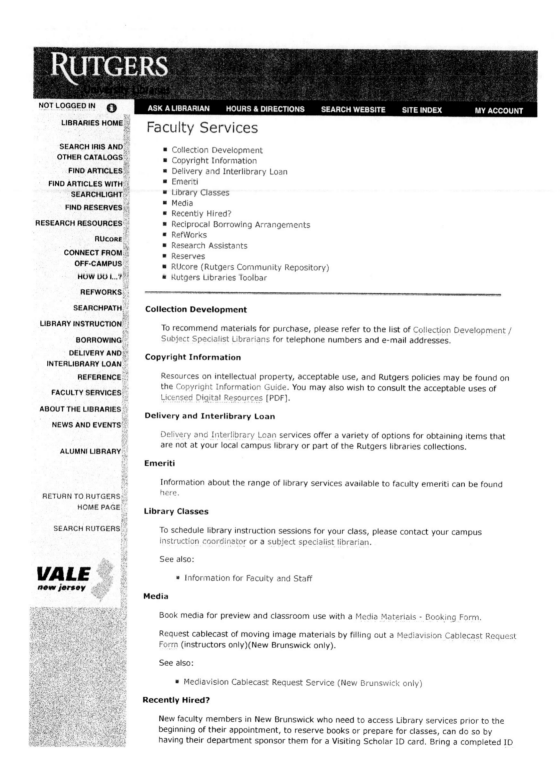

http://www.libraries.rutgers.edu/rul/lib_servs/faculty_services.shtml

Card Request Form [PDF], signed by your department head, to University Human Resources, ASB II, Cook Campus. Complete instructions are available at the Rutgers RUconnection Card website.

Faculty members in Newark should contact the Rutgers-Newark Photo ID Office. Camden faculty members should go to the IMPACT Booth in the Camden Campus Center.

Once you obtain your card, present it at any library circulation desk to activate borrowing privileges.

Reciprocal Borrowing Arrangements

To borrow from other academic institutions in the Tri-state area, please refer to policies on Cooperative Access Arrangements.

RefWorks

RefWorks is a Web-based bibliographic citation manager which works with most library databases.

Research Assistants

To designate a Research Assistant (RA) to checkout and renew books, request delivery of books and articles, and book media for classroom use on your behalf, request a Faculty Research Assistant (RA) Card.

Reserves

Place materials on reserve for a course by filling out a Reserve Request Form (instructors only).

See also:

- Reserve Services, A Guide for Faculty
- Electronic Documents on Reserve: A User's Guide

RUcore (Rutgers Community Repository)

RUcore is an open access institutional repository that makes the significant intellectual property of Rutgers University faculty and Rutgers University departments, centers, and institutes permanently and freely accessible for scholars and researchers around the globe.

Rutgers University faculties are invited to deposit the results of their research and professional activity. Your deposits will be preserved and made permanently available in RUcore. Articles resulting from NIH funding can be placed jointly in PubMed Central and RUcore easily via the RUL/NIH Submission Service.

Rutgers Libraries Toolbar

The Rutgers Libraries' Toolbar is a free web browser extension that provides a drop-down menu to library resources, embedded library links on certain popular web pages such as Amazon.com, and new functionality to the "right-click menu" of your mouse.

Last updated November 6, 2006; January 7, 2007; February 28, 2008
URL: http://www.libraries.rutgers.edu/rul/lib_servs/faculty_services.shtml
Send Website feedback to the Libraries Webmaster

School of Graduate and Postdoctoral Studies

The University of Western Ontario

Welcome!

The goal of graduate education is to transform students into scholars and professionals in their disciplines. The programs of the 360° degree graduate student professional development initiative provide critical communication, writing, and professional skills that enable new scholars to disseminate their research, to teach effectively and collaborate successfully, and provide career preparation that facilitates their successful transition to careers in academia, government, industry and beyond.

The 360° Graduate Student Professional Development Initiative is the result of campus-wide collaboration between the School of Graduate and Postdoctoral Studies, the Teaching Support Centre, Student Development Services, Western Libraries, the Career Centre, Communications and Public Affairs, the Faculties and many other colleagues across campus. Programs of the 360 Initiative are designed to complement the disciplinary preparation that graduate students receive in their departments through coursework, research, conference participation and interaction with faculty.

Navigation:
- Orientation Activities
- Teaching
- Research
- Mentoring
- Academic and Professional Communication
- International Grad Student Programs
- Career Development
- Campus Life

SEARCH

Online Resources
- Strategies for Academic Success
- Writing and Publication
- Teaching Tips
- Getting Mentored
- Career Resources
- Campus Community

Event Calendar

1151 Richmond Street, London, Ontario, Canada, N6A 3K7
Tel: 519-661-2111
Developed by The School of Graduate and Postdoctoral Studies Web Developer
See our policies on Privacy, and Web Standards

Western

Descriptions of Spaces

http://www.lib.uci.edu/libraries/study.html

UCI LIBRARIES
UNIVERSITY of CALIFORNIA · IRVINE

GO>

Home : Online Resources : Services : Libraries - Langson - Science - Grunigen Medical - Gateway Study Center

--- STUDY CENTERS & STUDY ROOMS ---

ASK A LIBRARIAN
Need Help? Click Here

Quick Links

LIBRARIES

• Hours
• Locations, Directions, & Parking
• Call Number Locations
• Contact Us
• Collections & Archives
• Library Publications
• Jobs
• Giving to the Libraries
• Exhibits
• What's New
• Policies
• Projects and Initiatives
• SCAMP - Scholarly Communication and Management Program

• **Langson Library**
• **Science Library**
• **Grunigen Medical Library**

• **Roger C. Holden Faculty and Graduate Student Reading Room (LL)**
• **Faculty and Graduate Reading Room (SL)**

Langson Library

• The Langson Library offers quiet study space in a wide range of options including 852 individual study spaces located primarily on the third, fourth, and basement floors.
• The 4th floor, Basement, Special Collections, and Southeast Asian Archive are designated Quiet Study Zones. Please turn your cell phones off and take all conversations outside.
• UCI faculty and graduate students may take advantage of the Roger C. Holden faculty and graduate student reading room.
• The Gateway Study Center, located across from the Langson Library, also provides a number of reader carrels in an environment dedicated to quiet study.

Gateway Study Center

The Gateway Study Center is located across from the Langson Library. The Study Center provides a number of carrels and library tables in an environment dedicated to quiet study.

• Open 24 hours pre-finals and finals week.
• The Study Center is a designated Quiet Zone.

Science Library

• The Science Library offers quiet study space in a wide range of options including 2000 individual study spaces located primarily on the fourth, fifth, and sixth floors, and over fifty study rooms of varying sizes which can be reserved in advance at the Directions Desk.
• The 4th, 5th and 6th floor Bar and Drum study halls are designated Quiet Study Zones. Please turn your cell phones off and take all conversations outside.
• The Science Library also has a Faculty and Graduate Reading Room on the fourth floor and a Study Center for after-hours studying on the first floor.

Science Library Study Center

The Science Library Study Center is located on the first floor of the Science Library. The Study Center may be entered from a separate outside entrance during times when the Library building is closed. A total of 110 individual study spaces are available to library users. For additional information please call, (949) 824-3681.

• There are nine Group Study Rooms within the Study Center. Group Study Rooms are located on the 1st, 4th, 5th, and 6th Floors. A total of 51 Group Study Rooms are available throughout the Science Library during normal hours of operation. Study room key checkouts and advance reservations are handled at the Directions Desk. Food is not allowed in the Study Rooms. Beverages in spill proof containers is acceptable. If you have food or beverages you will be asked to dispose of the items and/or asked to leave the library.
  ○ To avoid fines/blocks on your library record, please return/renew your room key on time.

- There will be $10 fine for overdue keys and a block will be placed on your circulation record.
- Please keep noise at a minimum level.
- Do not add or remove furniture.
- Do not deface, destroy, or vandalize walls or furniture. Disciplinary actions will be taken if you violate this rule.
- Open 24 hours pre-finals and finals week.
- The Study Center is a designated Quiet Zone.

Grunigen Medical Library

There is study space inside the library that may be used by all patrons.

Roger C. Holden Faculty and Graduate Student Reading Room (LL)

- The Roger C. Holden faculty and graduate student reading room is located on the second floor, LL 203.
- The Reading Room offers an attractive and comfortable space for UCI faculty and graduate students to conduct research in the library.
- The Reading Room includes quiet research space with study carrels, library tables, and two pcs. Please speak to a Loan Desk staff member for additional information on using this facility.

Faculty and Graduate Reading Room (SL)

- The Faculty and Graduate Reading Room is located on the Fourth Floor, SL 411 BAR.
- The Reading Room may be entered on either the fourth or fifth floors.
- UCI faculty and graduate students may use the reading room by checking out a cardkey from the Directions Desk.
- Cardkeys are non-renewable and should be returned on or before the assigned due date. Questions? Call (949) 824-3681

◀ Back

Top of Page ▲

University of California, Irvine • Irvine, CA 92623 - 9557 • 949.824.6836
© 2005 The Regents of the University of California. All Rights Reserved.
Last Updated: 11/14/2008 11:54:02
Comments and Suggestions : Privacy Statement

The University of Delaware Library

Home · DELCAT · Databases · Electronic Journals · Subjects A-Z · Forms · Reserves · Ask a Librarian

Library Retired Faculty Room

The University of Delaware provides access to a Retired Faculty Room on the Lower Level of the Morris Library for use by retirees of the University of Delaware.

- **USE OF ROOM:** The Library Retired Faculty Room 031 C on the lower level of the Morris Library has been made available for retirees of the University of Delaware to conduct library-related research and/or to provide professional space. The Library Retired Faculty Room can be used simultaneously by multiple retirees. It is wheelchair accessible. Beverages with lids or re-sealable beverages are permitted in the Library Retired Faculty Room. Food and smoking are not permitted. Library staff are not able to receive or deliver messages or mail to users of the Retired Faculty Room.

- **EQUIPMENT:** The room has been supplied with a computer with Internet access, Microsoft Office software, a printer, and a fax machine for self-service by retirees. Contact the Student Multimedia Design Center Desk with questions about the equipment in the room. If problems arise with the equipment, the concern should be reported to the Student Multimedia Design Center Desk, the Circulation Desk, or to Library Administration (Room 210).

- **ACCESS:** Library staff will ask to see University of Delaware photo identification cards before the key for the Library Retired Faculty Room is released, and the user will be requested to sign a usage in and out register.

- **KEYS:** Faculty may request a personal key for long-term use at the Library Administration Office (Room 210). Faculty may request a key for temporary use to be returned the same day from the Circulation Desk (First Floor) or at the Student Multimedia Design Center Desk (Lower Level). The key to the Library Retired Faculty Room should not be duplicated. A lost key should be reported to the location from which it was distributed as appropriate i.e. Student Multimedia Design Center Desk or Circulation Desk for temporary keys, and Library Administration for long term keys.

- **SECURITY:** Please keep the Retired Faculty Room locked when not in use. University insurance does not cover the contents of the Library Retired Faculty Room whether it is locked or unlocked. Please do not leave personal possessions or Library materials in the room. Contact the library service desk from which you picked up your key with any security-related question or problem.

When the use of the Library Retired Faculty Room is no longer needed, the key should be returned to the Library service desk from which it was distributed.

This page is maintained by Julia Hamm, Office of the Director.

Home · DELCAT · Databases · Electronic Journals · Subjects A-Z · Forms · Reserves · Ask a Librarian

UNIVERSITY OF DELAWARE LIBRARY

Graduate Student Carrels

The University of Delaware offers dedicated library research space for a limited time in the Morris Library to University of Delaware matriculated graduate students who have a valid University of Delaware I.D. There are 110 graduate carrels located on the lower level, second and third floors of the Morris Library. The carrels are:

- Assigned for one academic year, with the possibility of renewal by students who comply with the policies and procedures for use of the carrel.
- Assigned on a "first come, first served" basis.
- Assigned to two UD graduate students simultaneously, with each graduate student occupant assigned to his/her own unique locking shelf to store personal materials.
- Equipped with task lighting and data connectivity ready for use with the individual's laptop using a roaming IP address.

University of Delaware graduate students interested in obtaining a carrel may obtain the Application for Graduate Student Carrels from the Library Administration office, room 210 (second floor), or the Circulation Desk in the Morris Library. A copy of "*Library Graduate Student Carrels Policies and Procedures*" is given to each applicant and includes an application.

The completed application should be submitted to the Library Administration office, room 210 during standard office hours. Completed applications require the signature of the chairperson of his/her department or faculty advisor, endorsing their active graduate student status and the need for a carrel for library related research. Please call 831-2231 for additional information.

This page is maintained by Library Administrative Services.

Home · DELCAT · Databases · Electronic Journals · Subjects A-Z · Forms · Reserves · Ask a Librarian

http://web.uflib.ufl.edu/ps/Circ/graduatestudypolicies.html

University of Florida
George A. Smathers Libraries   Library Catalog | Databases | Site Map | Search

Graduate Study Carrel Policies

Library West has 84 graduate study carrels that contain a desk, chair, shelving, and wireless internet access. Assignments are made by the Library West Circulation Coordinator. Priority is given to currently enrolled graduate students with Social Sciences and Humanities majors completing their doctoral dissertations and masters theses. Graduate students with physical access disabilities will be given special consideration. A waiting list is maintained so that carrels that are relinquished during the year may be reassigned. The assignment period ends on the last day of the Summer C semester. Renewal of graduate study carrels is not automatic and reassignment is not guaranteed. Graduate students must re-apply before each Fall semester.

Procedure:

- Graduate students submit a Graduate Study Carrel Application Form online prior to the first week of Fall classes. This form is only for the carrels in Library West. Please inquire at the Circulation Desk of other libraries for their carrel procedures.

- The Library West Circulation Coordinator maintains the database of applicants and makes assignments after drop/add in the Fall.

- Graduate students are notified via email when assignments have been made. The key must be picked up in person at the Library West Circulation Desk and signed out by the assignee. An assignee with a disability may send instructions to release the key to a registered proxy.

- All personal books, papers, and other belongings must be removed and the key returned to the Library West Circulation Desk no later than the last day of the Summer C semester.

Guidelines For Use

- Graduate study carrels are available for use during all hours Library West is open.

- Assignees should not leave valuables or personal belongings that may be stolen or damaged; the security of the study carrel cannot be guaranteed.

- Drinks in covered containers are acceptable. Assignee is responsible for keeping trash empty; housekeeping staff do not enter carrels to remove trash or to clean surfaces of carpet.

- Study carrels are not soundproof. Please be considerate of other library users.

- Library furniture from other locations may not be moved into study carrels.

- Library materials kept in carrels must be checked out to the graduate student. Library staff regularly monitor study carrels and will remove any library materials not properly checked out. Library materials located in study carrels are subject to overdue notices, recalls, and other library policies.

- Appliances that pose fire hazards – heaters, coffee pots, etc. – are strictly prohibited.

- For security, keys may not be duplicated. There is a $35.00 replacement charge for lost keys.

- Lights should be turned off and doors securely locked when leaving the study room.

- Library privileges will be blocked if the key is not returned by the last day of the Summer C semester. There is a non-refundable $35.00 replacement charge if the key is not returned after notification of expiration.

- Names of assignees are confidential and will not be released without a court order.

- Repeat violations of guidelines may result in revocation of the study carrel.

University of Florida
George A. Smathers Libraries   Library Catalog | Databases | Site Map | Search

Faculty Study Room Policies

Library West has 36 individually assigned faculty study rooms that are furnished with a desk, chair, and book shelf and that provide wireless internet access. The assignment period is for one academic year, beginning at the end of the first week of classes during fall semester and ending on the last day of the Summer C semester. Any current University of Florida faculty member who is in social science or humanities fields and who is at the rank of Assistant Professor or above may apply for a study. Priority will be given first to those on sabbatical who are using the resources of Library West and second to those at the rank of Assistant Professor. The Library West Circulation Coordinator makes study assignments, using a lottery if there are more applicants than studies in the priority categories. A waiting list will be maintained so that studies relinquished early may be reassigned.

Procedure:

∴ Faculty submit a Faculty Study Room Application Form online anytime prior to the first week of Fall classes.

∴ The Library West Circulation Coordinator maintains the database of applicants and makes assignments after drop/add in the Fall.

∴ Access Services notifies all faculty applicants via email when assignments have been made.

∴ Faculty with studies must pick up their key in person at the Library West Circulation Desk. An assignee with a disability may send instructions to release the key to a registered proxy.

∴ Faculty must remove all personal books, papers, and other belongings and return the key to the Library West Circulation Desk no later than the last day of Summer C semester.

Guidelines For Use

∴ Faculty study rooms are available for use during all hours Library West is open.

∴ For security, study room keys may not be duplicated. There is a $35.00 replacement charge for lost keys.

∴ Names of assignees are confidential and will not be released without a court order.

∴ Library furniture from other locations may not be moved into study rooms.

∴ Library materials kept in study rooms must be checked out to the faculty member. Library staff regularly monitor study rooms and will remove any library materials not properly checked out. Library materials located in study rooms are treated the same as materials taken to the faculty member's home or office; that is, they are subject to overdue notices, recalls, and other library policies.

∴ Drinks in covered containers are acceptable. Assignee is responsible for keeping trash empty; housekeeping staff do not enter carrels to remove trash or to clean surfaces of carpet.

∴ Appliances that pose fire hazards – heaters, coffee pots, etc. – are strictly prohibited.

∴ Study rooms are not soundproof. Please be considerate of other library users.

∴ Lights should be turned off and doors securely locked when leaving the study room.

∴ Assignees should not leave valuables or personal belongings that may be stolen or damaged; the security of the study room cannot be guaranteed.

∴ Library privileges will be blocked if the key is not returned by the last day of the Summer C semester. There is a non-refundable $35.00 replacement charge if the key is not returned after notification of expiration.

Library Services > Study Areas > Lockmobiles

Lockmobiles

Lockmobiles are wheeled, lockable carts that offer convenient, safe storage for books, papers, and other research materials when you're not in the Library. They also make it easier to gather books and periodicals from the stacks, make photocopies, etc. Lockmobiles are available for use by GW graduate students (except Law and Medical School students).

Lockmobiles are intended for use by graduate students who are engaged in research projects that require heavy use of library materials. Lockmobiles are offered as an alternative to the use of a closed study room.

To apply for or renew use of a lockmobile, print out the Lockmobile Application Form. You will need to have the form signed by a faculty advisor or department chair. Return the completed form to Barbra Tschida at the Circulation Desk on 1st floor in Gelman Library. There is a $10 deposit required for lockmobile use.

You will need to renew your lockmobile for each semester you intend to use it.

Lockmobiles are extremely popular and often all available units are reserved.

If you have questions, contact Barbra Tschida, Circulation and Reserves Group Leader, (202) 994-1336, btschida@gwu.edu.

THE GEORGE
WASHINGTON
UNIVERSITY
WASHINGTON DC

Last modified: Friday, September 15, 2006 15:55:54 PM

LIBRARIES
INDIANA UNIVERSITY
Bloomington

The Research Commons:
A Concept for the Wells Library East Tower

Within the long process of research, from discovery to dissemination, scholars rely on institutional support. Indiana University, committed to its dual mission of advancing research and teaching, now has an unparalleled opportunity to aid research in a way that positions the university at the forefront of its peers and as a leader in the nation.

Creation of the Research Commons in the Herman B Wells Library will offer support—in one central campus location—to faculty and graduate students at any point in the complex research process. By assembling groups and expertise now distributed throughout the Bloomington campus, the Research Commons will blend technology with traditional resources to serve as a center for a wide range of scholarly activities.

Perhaps most important, faculty and graduate students from all disciplines will know that whatever their research needs, they can start at the Research Commons. They will no longer have to determine where to go on campus or whom to ask even the most basic questions, from "How do I get started?" or "How do I digitize and archive this?" to "How do I copyright my work?". By providing a space for collaboration and information-sharing, the Research Commons will help faculty and graduate students benefit from the tools and techniques already put in place by their colleagues in other disciplines. Moreover, the collective expertise of librarians and technologists will help them realize the true potential of the vast information resources of Indiana University.

The Research Commons will leverage three established strengths:

Expertise

Perhaps the greatest promise of the Research Commons will be its ability to draw together many layers of expertise in one location. Services provided by units now on campus—and other services yet to be introduced—will be combined in a singular destination. Researchers will benefit from a transparent delivery of services, whether they are looking for guidance in reference and research services, metadata creation, grants and sponsored research, statistical analysis, or one of many other areas essential to their work. Librarians, technologists, consultants, designers, and developers from many campus units will all contribute to this effort. Success will depend on the leadership of the IUB Libraries, UITS and OVPR, and build on their longstanding partnership.

Expertise will also be shared among researchers. The final report of the IU Cyberinfrastructure Research Taskforce points to the value of bringing together researchers who may be unaware of the tools and techniques used by scholars in other disciplines. "Chemists and physicists struggle with the complexity of national cyberinfrastructure efforts, such as the TeraGrid," the report states, "while other scholars wrestle with the complexities of evolving desktop tools." As a place for community-building, the Research Commons will address the need for scholars to interrelate, both within and across the conventional boundaries of their disciplines.

The Research Commons will increase efficiencies not only for researchers who may value a central point for sharing information, but also for the disparate units of a complex university, where one unit often recreates or duplicates what is offered by another.

Infrastructure

Just as scientists need laboratories, researchers in every discipline need environments designed and equipped to meet their scholarly needs. The Herman B Wells Library offers essential space in a prime campus location. The entire East Tower of the Wells Library, with floor space greater than 11 football fields, will be dedicated to the Research Commons.

Technology will be an essential and conspicuous component of the Research Commons, with equipment necessary to support a wide range of scholarly activity. The Research Commons will provide a scholars laboratory that will serve as a resource for digital media production and archiving. Other dedicated space will accommodate high-performance computing, statistical and mathematical services and software, database support, and visualization. Collaborative technologies that allow people separated by hundreds or thousands of miles to interact as naturally as if they were together in a meeting room are now of genuine value to scholars in any discipline.

Key to the success of the Research Commons will be balancing the space for active collaboration and computing with quiet space essential for reading or contemplation. A redesigned reading room on the first floor, for example, will provide a well-lit inspirational environment for individual work. Centers for research expertise will be integrated on floors with their complementary collections. Shared space will encourage community-building within and across disciplines. Seminar rooms will offer space for faculty to form and develop ideas.

A suite of online services will accompany these physical spaces. By accessing information and services through an online portal, scholars will not have to be in the Wells Library to experience many of the benefits of the Research Commons.

Information Resources

A research library—the traditional locus for scholars to interact among the collections they value—can offer similar opportunities in a digital age. The rich collections of the IUB Libraries will be a central feature of the Research Commons. Priority will be given to services and spaces in direct support of print and digital collections. The Wells Library is home to the books, journals, microfiche, films, and other materials that researchers, particularly in the humanities and social sciences, rely upon for their scholarly needs.

In many disciplines, electronic collections and data sets are essential. Government statistics, now available online, can be sorted and manipulated in ways not possible just a few years ago. Software, including IU-licensed software, will be broadly available. Partnering units will offer their own specialized databases, programs, and information resources.

* * *

By investing in this concept for the Research Commons in the Wells Library, Indiana University now has the opportunity to address key needs voiced by its research faculty, leverage established strengths, and increase organizational efficiencies. Creation of the Research Commons will advance the university's core mission and signal a major commitment to researchers in all disciplines.

INDIANA UNIVERSITY BLOOMINGTON: The Research Commons: Planning Library Space and Services...

http://www.cni.org/tfms/2007b.fall/Abstracts/presentations/cni-research-steele.ppt

11/14/08

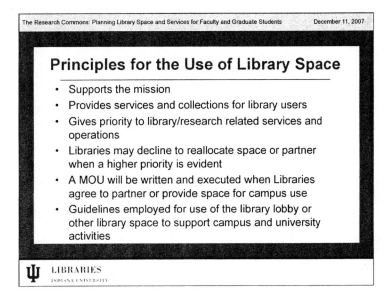

1

INDIANA UNIVERSITY BLOOMINGTON: The Research Commons: Planning Library Space and Services...

http://www.cni.org/tfms/2007b.fall/Abstracts/presentations/cni-research-steele.ppt

11/14/08

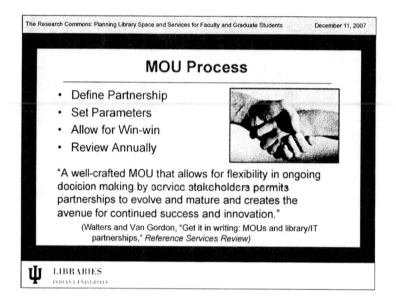

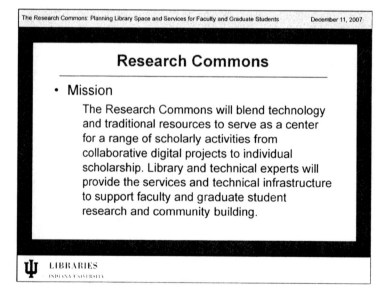

INDIANA UNIVERSITY BLOOMINGTON: The Research Commons: Planning Library Space and Services...

http://www.cni.org/tfms/2007b.fall/Abstracts/presentations/cni-research-steele.ppt

11/14/08

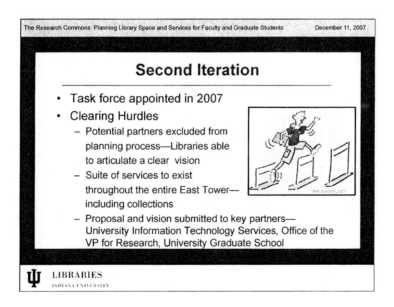

3

INDIANA UNIVERSITY BLOOMINGTON: The Research Commons: Planning Library Space and Services...

http://www.cni.org/tfms/2007b.fall/Abstracts/presentations/cni-research-steele.ppt

11/14/08

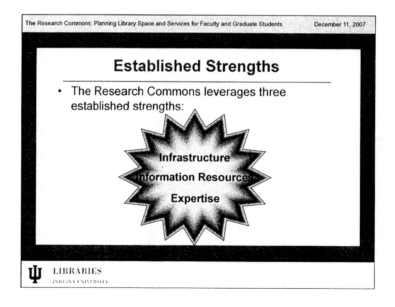

4

INDIANA UNIVERSITY BLOOMINGTON: The Research Commons: Planning Library Space and Services...

http://www.cni.org/tfms/2007b.fall/Abstracts/presentations/cni-research-steele.ppt

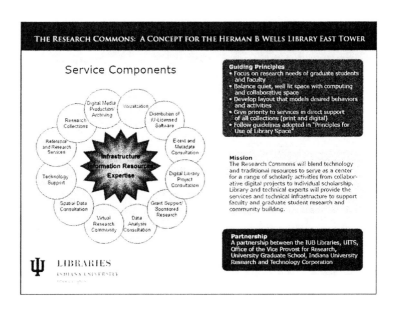

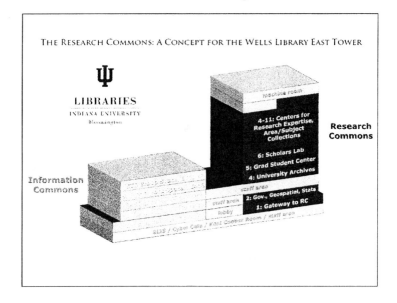

INDIANA UNIVERSITY BLOOMINGTON: The Research Commons: Planning Library Space and Services...

http://www.cni.org/tfms/2007b.fall/Abstracts/presentations/cni-research-steele.ppt

11/14/08

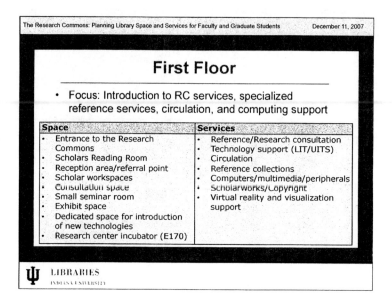

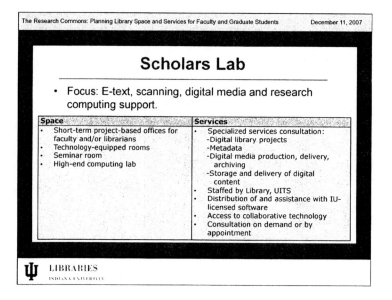

INDIANA UNIVERSITY BLOOMINGTON: The Research Commons: Planning Library Space and Services...

http://www.cni.org/tfms/2007b.fall/Abstracts/presentations/cni-research-steele.ppt

11/14/08

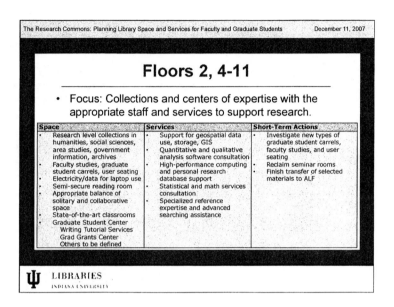

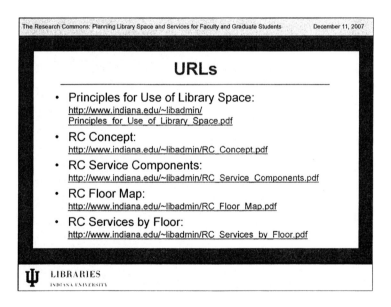

7

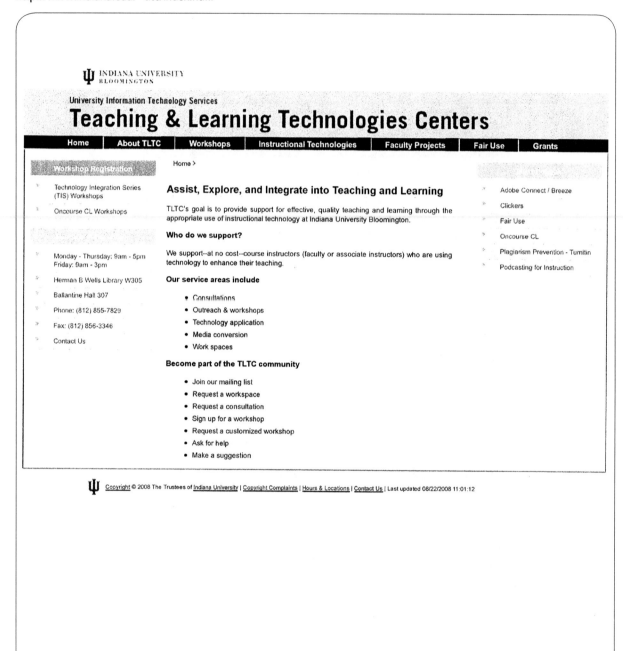

INDIANA UNIVERSITY
BLOOMINGTON

University Information Technology Services

Teaching & Learning Technologies Centers

| Home | About TLTC | Workshops | Instructional Technologies | Faculty Projects | Fair Use | Grants |

Workshop Registration

- Technology Integration Series (TIS) Workshops
- Oncourse CL Workshops

Monday - Thursday: 9am - 5pm
Friday: 9am - 3pm

- Herman B Wells Library W305
- Ballantine Hall 307
- Phone: (812) 855-7829
- Fax: (812) 856-3346
- Contact Us

Home >

Assist, Explore, and Integrate into Teaching and Learning

TLTC's goal is to provide support for effective, quality teaching and learning through the appropriate use of instructional technology at Indiana University Bloomington.

Who do we support?

We support--at no cost--course instructors (faculty or associate instructors) who are using technology to enhance their teaching.

Our service areas include

- Consultations
- Outreach & workshops
- Technology application
- Media conversion
- Work spaces

Become part of the TLTC community

- Join our mailing list
- Request a workspace
- Request a consultation
- Sign up for a workshop
- Request a customized workshop
- Ask for help
- Make a suggestion

- Adobe Connect / Breeze
- Clickers
- Fair Use
- Oncourse CL
- Plagiarism Prevention - Turnitin
- Podcasting for Instruction

OHIO UNIVERSITY *Libraries*

ALICE | InfoTree | home

ASK A LIBRARIAN ▶ im | chat | phone | e-mail

| Find | Services | Collections | Library Info |

Faculty Commons –
*provides support for teaching,
scholarship and engagement*

The Floor Plan
Calendar of Events

The Big Idea

The Big Picture

Affiliates

Campus-Community Engagement
Center for Academic Technology
Center for Teaching & Learning
Center for Writing Excellence
Library Collection Development
Media Production

Why a Faculty Commons?

Provost Krendl's desire for better and more pervasive faculty support coincided with the necessity of finding new space for three units that support faculty teaching: the former Center for Innovations in Technology for Learning (CITL), now the Center for Academic Technology (CAT); the Center for Teaching Excellence, now the Center for Teaching and Learning (CTL); and the Center for Writing Excellence (CWE). Currently these offices are housed in a hard-to-find location in the basement of Scott Quad, which is slated for conversion into residence hall space. And thus, the idea for a "Faculty Commons" to be housed in Alden library was born.

Importantly, the University's strategic plan, Vision Ohio, emphasizes excellence in teaching undergraduate students, and the purpose of CAT, CTE, and CWE is to support and collaborate with faculty on best teaching practices, innovative classroom approaches, making the best of our students' learning, as well as supporting research and scholarship, primarily the scholarship of teaching and learning. It seemed logical that a new and more convenient location for these units would increase the visibility and use of these important resources. Likewise, Alden Library's IMTS, now known as Media Production, has a long history of supporting faculty teaching and scholarship needs by providing graphic art and multi-media creation services to faculty. In a move from the second to the third floor, Media Production will be a prominent member of the Faculty Commons as well.

The success of the Student Learning Commons gives us hope that bringing together faculty in a similarly conceived space where they can find support for their teaching and scholarship as well as a place to relax and share a cup of coffee, will meet some previously unmet needs of the faculty. Many academic libraries are reinventing themselves, and while continuing to provide traditional resources like books, journals, study space, and reference services, they are becoming centers for many types of academic services. And why not? Libraries are "neutral territory" and belong to everyone; they are open long hours; and they are focused on student and faculty success. The synergies between library services and other academic activities are obvious. We welcome the Faculty Commons, and you, to the third floor of Alden Library.

By Julia Zimmerman

Archives & Special Collections   International Collections   Health Sciences   Music & Dance

OHIO University Libraries
Athens, OH 45701-2978
Phone: (740) 593-2978

Last updated: May 22, 2008
This page is maintained by Kate Anderson.
Please use our Feedback Form for your questions, comments, and suggestions about the Libraries' services and resources.

OHIO UNIVERSITY *Libraries*

ALICE | InfoTree | home

ASK A LIBRARIAN ▶ im | chat | phone | e-mail

| Find | Services | Collections | Library Info |

Faculty Commons –
provides support for teaching, scholarship and engagement

The Floor Plan
Calendar of Events
The Big Idea

The Big Picture

Affiliates
Campus-Community Engagement
Center for Academic Technology
Center for Teaching & Learning
Center for Writing Excellence
Library Collection Development
Media Production

What is the Faculty Commons?

The Faculty Commons is projected to open in September, 2007. Approximately 9000 square feet on the third floor of Alden library has been designated for this innovative space. In addition to providing a home for the Center for Academic Technology (CAT), the Center for Teaching and Learning (CTL), and the Center for Writing Excellence (CWE), the Commons will house Media Production (formerly IMTS Graphics, photography and Multimedia), which provides a variety of graphic art and multi-media creation services to faculty. The chief collection development officer, who oversees liaison activities between librarians and faculty, will have an office in the Faculty Commons as well.

These offices, along with three well-equipped conference rooms for faculty use, will surround a large, open, lobby-like space that contains workstations, desks and tables, and soft seating. In focus groups, in addition to support for teaching and scholarship, faculty asked for a quiet place to read and study in Alden Library, and the Commons provides an ideal space for these activities. On the other hand, a coffee bar and coffee kiosk offer faculty much needed social space. The new conference rooms are ideal for meetings and for the seminars and workshops provided by the CAT, CTL, and CWE.

Display areas, both high-tech and traditional, will showcase faculty research and teaching projects. Finally, a state-of-the-art technology-equipped classroom—a renovation of the Friends of the Library Room on the 3rd floor—is also included in the project.

Funding, which comes from the Provost, the Libraries, CAT, CTE, and CWE, Media Production, and the University's renovation budget, underscores the collaborative nature of the project.

The Faculty Commons is another step in the Library Master Plan, which lays out plans for a total renovation of Alden Library. This highly innovative approach will provide high-quality work and study space for faculty, along with services essential to excellent instruction and scholarship, meeting the goals of the library, faculty development, and the university as a whole.

Archives & Special Collections   International Collections   Health Sciences   Music & Dance

OHIO University Libraries
Athens, OH 45701-2978
Phone: (740) 593-2699

Last updated: May 22, 2008
This page is maintained by Kate Anderson.
Please use our **Feedback Form** for your questions, comments, and suggestions about the Libraries' services and resources.

OHIO UNIVERSITY: Faculty Commons: one stop service resources

http://www.library.ohiou.edu/fc/

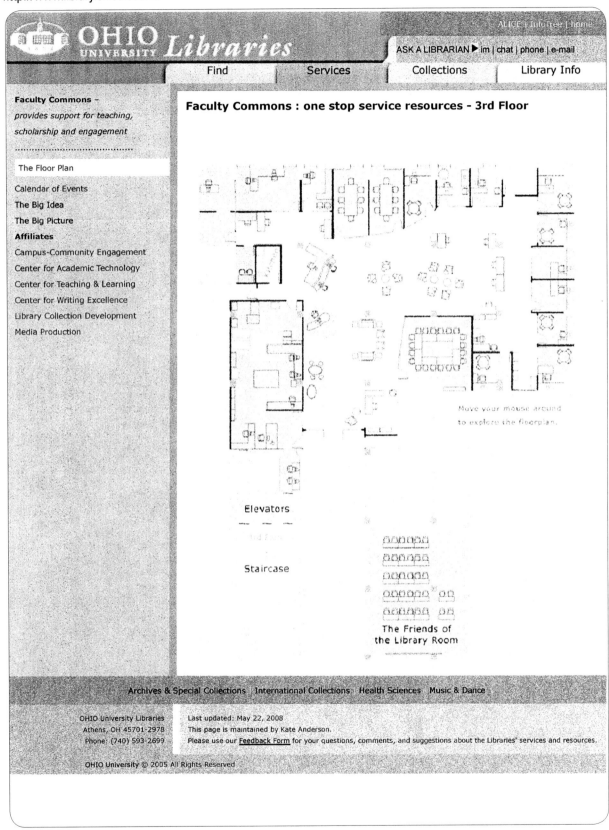

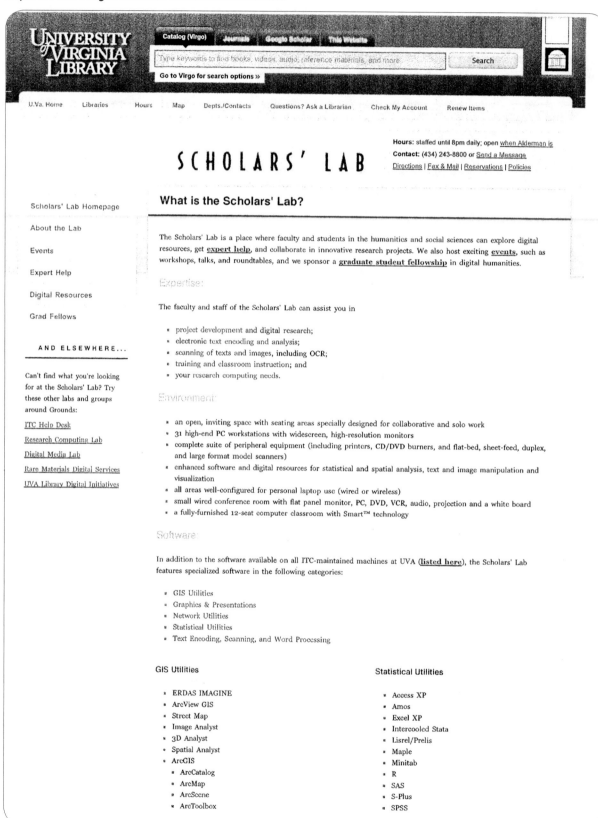

- Spatial Analyst
- Geostatistical Analyst
- 3D Analyst

Graphics and Presentations

- Adobe Photoshop
- Adobe ImageReady
- Microsoft PowerPoint
- GeoExpress View (Mr. SID viewer)
- Dreamweaver

Network Utilities (E-Mail, HomeDir, etc.)

- Corporate Time for the Web
- Exceed
- Home Directory
- Internet Explorer
- Mulberry
- Mozilla
- Secure CRT
- Secure FX
- WinZip

- Stat Transfer
- Stata

Text Encoding, Scanning, and Word Processing

- ABBYY FineReader OCR
- Adobe Acrobat Professional
- Acrobat Distiller
- Microsoft Word
- NoteTab
- OmniPage Professional OCR
- oXygen XML Editor

UNIVERSITY *of* VIRGINIA LIBRARY

Research Computing Lab

Hours: Mon-Thurs 8am-12am, Fri 8am-9pm,
Sat 10am-6pm, Sun 10am-12am
Contact: (434) 243-8799 or Send a Help Request
Staff | Map | Mailing Address

Inspiring innovation in science and engineering

The Research Computing Lab is a collaborative partnership between ITC's Research Computing Support Group and the Brown Science and Engineering Library. The purpose of this partnership is to provide a convenient space for faculty and students to work on innovative projects with specialists and get support for instruction and research in the science and engineering disciplines.

We offer consultation services in a wide variety of technologies and methodologies for high performance and research computing. We provide support services in person, via phone, and through our web help ticket system. Our business hours cater to the researcher, professional, instructor, and student.

News

HPC "Tiger Team Program" now available through UVACSE

UVa at Forefront of High Performance Humanities

more news...

Events

NOV. 17 — "Visualization" with Kirsten Miles

NOV. 18 — "Numerical Methods Using R" with Kathy Gerber

NOV. 18 — "LabView Users Group Meeting"

more events...

Consultation Services

Usability and User Requirements Services

Distributed Software

Lab Hardware

Lab Software

Digital Collections

Collaborative Projects

Book Collection

Related Websites

Specialists

- **Scientific Computing**
  Kathy Gerber
- **G.I.S.**
  Kelly Johnston
- **Metadata**
  Sherry Lake
- **Usability Testing**
  Erin Mayhood

University of Virginia Library
PO Box 400115, Charlottesville, VA 22904-4113

Libraries | Depts./Contacts | U.Va. Home | ITC
Website Feedback | Search | Questions? Ask a Librarian | Hours | Map | Policies | Press | Jobs

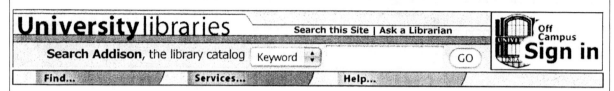

Graduate Study Room

The Graduate Study Room (416 Newman) is a space reserved for graduate students to study and relax. Access is limited through the Hokie Passport, which must be swiped before the door will open. (If your Hokie Passport soes not open the door, contact the Graduate School.)

Lockers are available for free checkout. Stop in the Dean's Suite on the 6th floor to reserve one.

Return to floor maps of the Library

Last updated: 7/14/08 by Robert Sebek

DEPOSITORY
LIBRARY

University Libraries
Virginia Tech
P.O. Box 90001
Blacksburg, VA 24062-9001
540-231-6170

Direction to libraries

http://www.lib.vt.edu/help/direct/tour/floor4/gradroom.html

Position Description

Oklahoma State University
Library

ANNOUNCING
Victor Dominguez Baeza
Director, Library Graduate
& Research Services

Victor Dominguez Baeza is an associate professor and Director of Library Graduate and Research Services. In addition to teaching an undergraduate Library and Internet Information Competencies course at OSU, he provides leadership to the OSU Libraries in the areas of services, resources and training for faculty and graduate students. His 12 years of involvement in library instruction has given him diverse experience in designing, directing and delivering workshops, training sessions and seminars to the academic community. Victor holds a BS with honors in Communication from Eastern New Mexico University, a MBA from Texas Christian University and a MLS from the University of North Texas.

Oklahoma State University
Library

ANNOUNCING

Victor
Dominguez
Baeza

Director, Library Graduate
& Research Services

Contact:

306 Library
victor.baeza@okstate.edu
405-744-1241

Victor Baeza
Primary Assignment 2006*

Graduate Student and New Faculty Support. Develop and coordinate library programs supporting graduate students and new faculty members in utilizing library resources. Serve as the Library's liaison with the Graduate College and the Graduate and Professional Student Government Association to share information and develop new library programs and services. Coordinate efforts to inform faculty and graduate students about developments in scholarly communications, copyright, and intellectual property law.

Reference Service. Provide 6-8 hours of reference service at the General Reference desk including giving directions, helping patrons locate materials, and instructing patrons in the use of indexes, electronic reference tools, and other reference and bibliographic tools.

Collection Development/ Faculty Liaison. Perform collection development and liaison activities in the areas of Finance and Management Science and Information Systems.

Library Instruction. Participate in the general bibliographic instruction and library orientation services as needed within the Library.

Administrative Duties. Serve as a member of the Library Advisory Committee.

And other duties as assigned

* Will remain in effect until modified

Marketing and Outreach

Faculty *Library* Connection

Services for new BYU faculty

The Harold B. Lee Library is ready to serve your needs as an educator and as a research scholar. Please let us know what we can do for you.

Your subject librarian is:

Office: _____
Phone: _____
E-mail: _____

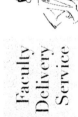

Faculty Delivery Service

The Interlibrary Loan Office provides a book delivery and retrieval service to faculty members. Faculty may also request items from other libraries through Interlibrary Loan. Books are delivered free of charge while articles and other copied materials can be delivered to you electronically as PDF files for $1.25 (the same price for paper copies up to 10 pages; 10 cents per page thereafter).

The charges are billed to your signature card account. The Library will pick up and return your checked-out items when you are finished with them. Books checked-out from our collection can be renewed online at http://www.lib.byu.edu/account.html. Contact Faculty Delivery Service at 422-5282 or fdds@byu.edu

Library Tour

To help your students improve their research skills they need to learn how the library works. We offer audio tours in MP3 format, online tutorials, research aids, and virtual maps of the library, as well as in-library classes.

For lectures that would benefit from the use of rare materials, we now offer a seminar room inside the secure area of Special Collections where you and your class can meet with a curator and look at ancient, rare, and influential artifacts from the vaults.

Course Reserve

Course Reserve helps your provide your students access to the books, lectures, streaming videos, photographs, and scholarly works.

Course Reserve helps you provide your students access to the books, lectures, streaming videos, photographs, and scholarly works that support your courses. Students can find traditional print materials such as books at the circulation desk in the library and can access the digital content you provide from any computer with an Internet connection.

To post materials on Course Reserve you can use the faculty request form we provide online at lib.byu.edu/fac_guide.html#reserve. For information on adding print or video materials to Course Reserve call us at 422-3745 or contact your subject librarian.

Database Access

As a faculty member you have access to thousands of scholarly databases using your library log in. You can access these databases anywhere you have Internet access.

We encourage you to take full advantage of this service and to share it with your students. To learn more about databases in your area of expertise contact your subject librarian.

Institutional Repository

The library can host your scholarly publications and research materials in a secure and accessible environment using D-space, the academic community's scholarly material management system.

Our Institutional Repository can host your digital artifacts such as books, photographs, video, and research data sets. Studies show that professors who place their materials in the Institutional Repository are cited more frequently.

Contact your subject librarian or Jeff Belliston, the Scholarly Communication Librarian, at Jeffrey_Belliston@byu.edu or Rebekah Sykes at rebekah_sykes@byu.edu.

RSS Feeds, Blogs, & My Library

Learn about new books and materials in your subject area by subscribing to our RSS feeds at lib.byu.edu/rss/index.php

Subject librarians also blog about new services and materials in the library. Visit lib.byu.edu/education/ or lib.byu.edu/business/

You can create your own custom library research page featuring your most valuable sources. Visit http://mylibrary.lib.byu.edu/

Faculty Research Rooms

The Library has research rooms for faculty who need space and privacy for scholarly work. Apply for a research room at lib.byu.edu/fac_research.html

www.lib.byu.edu/rss/index.php   www.lib.byu.edu/education or lib.byu.edu/business/   mylibrary.lib.byu.edu/

UCI Libraries Update
A Newsletter for Faculty

Volume 26, Number 2, Winter 2008

Volume 26, Number 2, Winter 2008

1 | 2 | 3 | 4 | 5 | 6 | Next

Library Endowed Funds Established

The Libraries have received two major gifts in the name of donors who are familiar to many at UCI: Ralph W. Gerard, one of UCI's founding Deans, and Sylvia Holden Robb, a dedicated supporter of UCI research and the Libraries for over 20 years.

The Ralph W. Gerard Reading Room was named last May in recognition of a gift from the Ralph W. & Leona B. Gerard Family Trust. Dr. Gerard, who died in 1974, was a revered neurophysiologist and behavioral scientist, known for his wide-ranging work on the nervous system, psycho-pharmacology, and the biological bases of schizophrenia. At the pinnacle of his career, he served as Founding Dean of the Graduate Division from 1963 to 1970 and Professor of Biological Sciences. The Ralph W. Gerard Library Endowed Fund will provide support to maintain and enhance the excellence of the Libraries' collections, services, and facilities.

Dr. Gerard and Mrs. Robb were dedicated to supporting scholarship and learning, and they understood the vital role the Libraries play in the impressive research and education taking place at UCI.

A second gift was received from the estate of the late Sylvia Holden Robb. Mrs. Robb, who died in 2006 at the age of 97, was a dedicated and generous supporter of the Libraries for over 20 years. Her many gifts to the Libraries include the naming of the Roger C. Holden Graduate and Faculty Reading Room in Langson Library and the establishment of the Sylvia Holden Robb Library Collections Fund. This latest gift establishes the Sylvia Holden Robb Library Endowed Fund, which provides general support to the Libraries.

These two important gifts create a permanent legacy of the impact these thoughtful donors have had on research and instruction at UCI. Dr. Gerard and Mrs. Robb were dedicated to supporting scholarship and learning, and they understood the vital role the Libraries play in the impressive research and teaching taking place at UCI. Their gifts help ensure the continuing excellence of the Libraries.

Top of page | Library Newsletters | UCI Libraries website

Inside this issue

Library Endowed Funds Established

New Interlibrary Loan Request Features

Library Speaker Series Features Ron Carlson

World Bank e-Library & SourceOECD

Library Recruitments

Special Collections and Archives on the Web

UCI Libraries Update

Contributors:
Jackie Dooley, Collette Ford, Pam La Zarr, Stephen MacLeod, Julie Sully, Daniel Tsang

Editor: Jackie Dooley

Design & Production: Sage Kim

COLUMBIA UNIVERSITY LIBRARIES

@ YOUR SERVICE

FACULTY GUIDE TO THE COLUMBIA UNIVERSITY LIBRARIES

"Columbia's Libraries are second to none. The online search capability, the responsiveness of staff, and the professionalism of all involved create an atmosphere where scholarship can thrive and students can learn. I am proud to be affiliated with an institution that recognizes the return on investment from an outstanding library system."

---Steven Schinke, Professor
Columbia University School of Social Work

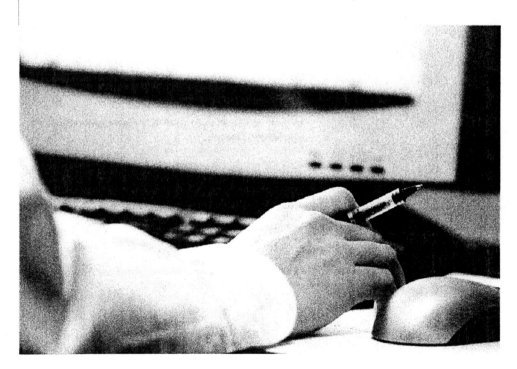

How the Libraries Work for You

Librarian Subject Specialists

Contact a librarian specializing in your field to recommend items for purchase, to receive in-depth assistance with research, or to request an instruction session for your students.
www.columbia.edu/library/subject_specialists

Research Consultations

Sign up for a one-on-one personalized session with a librarian subject specialist in your field—whether it's for guidance on a new project or assurance that you haven't missed anything as you research.

Request It—Borrow Direct & Interlibrary Loan

Looking for a book that's not available on campus? If the book or other material you need is checked out or not owned by the library, you can request it through Borrow Direct or Interlibrary Loan (ILL).
www.columbia.edu/library/borrow_direct
www.columbia.edu/library/ill

E-Resources from Off Campus

Using your Columbia ID (UNI) and password, you can access nearly all of our 1,000 online databases from anywhere in the world. Because the library pays for access to these resources, be sure to connect through the Libraries' website or to use the special "resolver URL"—e.g. *http://www.columbia.edu/cgi-bin/cul/resolve?lweb0051*—as found on the Databases webpage.
Find the database you need at **www.columbia. edu/library/databases**.

New E-Resources and Books Lists

Sign up to receive notice of new electronic additions to the collection at **www.columbia.edu/library/new_ eresources** and check **www.columbia.edu/library/ new_books** for a list of new books.

Suggest a Title for Purchase

Recommend a title for the Libraries online at **www.columbia.edu/library/ recommend**, or speak directly to your subject specialist.

Specialty Services

Electronic Text Service (ETS)
315 Butler Library
Hardware and software for producing and editing electronic texts and images; tools for textual analysis and document and citation management; an in-house collection of digitized primary source materials; and assistance in identifying and using online full-text resources are all available at ETS. An expert staff is always on hand to assist you.
www.columbia.edu/library/ets

Electronic Data Service (EDS)
215 Lehman Library
EDS, run jointly by CUIT and the Libraries, offers a rich data library, consulting services, and analysis tools to support instruction and research involving numeric and geospatial data resources.
www.columbia.edu/acis/eds

Butler Media Center
208B Butler Library
The newly upgraded equipment in this facility supports the playback of a collection of more than 12,000 feature films, documentaries, ethnographic films, and performing arts titles in multiple visual formats, including VHS (NTSC, PAL, and SECAM), DVDs, and laser discs. Refer to the website for information on access, circulation policies, and faculty services.
www.columbia.edu/library/bmc

The Music & Arts Library
701 Dodge Hall
In addition to its extensive book and music score collection, the library offers piano keyboards, audio and video viewing stations, audio, MIDI, and music notation software, and a collection of over 20,000 recordings, available for faculty to check out.
www.columbia.edu/library/music

HOW THE LIBRARIES WORK FOR YOUR STUDENTS

Targeted Instruction for Courses

Librarian subject specialists are available to provide customized research instruction for specific courses, in the classroom or in the library. To get started, visit **www.columbia.edu/library/ask**, or contact your subject specialist.

Course Reserves

Make the required reading for your classes easily available to your students. Include books, articles, audio or video materials, or e-resources. For more information on Course Reserves policies and contact information for each library, please visit **www.columbia.edu/library/reserves**.

CourseWorks: Research Guides

Your CourseWorks page can point your students not only to reserve readings, but also to other relevant library resources and services. If you're interested in learning more, e-mail **researchguides@libraries.cul.columbia.edu**.

Research Consultations

As your students begin projects or assist you, they can sign up for a one-on-one personalized research session with a librarian who specializes in your field. **www.columbia.edu/library/ask**

ADDITIONAL SERVICES

Downloading Tools and Plug-ins for Your Laptop

Streamline your research—download search or citation management tools (e.g., EndNote) and more. **www.columbia.edu/library/download**

Spouse ID Privileges

Your spouse or domestic partner can have borrowing privileges at all Morningside Campus libraries free of charge. Register together, with your Columbia ID and documentation of partnership or marriage, at the Library Information Office, 201 Butler. More information is available at **www.columbia.edu/library/lio**.

Deputy Borrowers

Faculty members can authorize up to three students, or other noncasual employees, to borrow materials directly from the libraries on their behalf. More information is available at **www.columbia.edu/library/lio**.

The Columbia University Libraries offer a wide variety of support for research and teaching—in the library, the classroom, and online. As always, we welcome faculty members to visit the Libraries to learn more about what's available to them. Discover our services, our staff, and more at

www.columbia.edu/library.

"Through instruction with librarians, my students are equipped to mine the literature and build a collaborative database that contributes value to my entire research group. Researchers from all disciplines should tap into the expertise and knowledge of the library staff and take advantage of the tremendous potential offered by the Libraries' electronic resources."

—Nicholas Turro, William P. Schweitzer Professor of Chemistry

"The Columbia Libraries attract scholars and students from every part of the globe while serving as essential foundation for the local needs of one of America's leading educational and research institutions. To be a scholar with daily access to the Columbia Libraries is to have at one's fingertips a rare wealth of resources for research, teaching, and learning."

—Robert Hymes, Chair of the Department of
East Asian Languages and Cultures and
H. Walpole Carpentier Professor of Chinese History

COLUMBIA UNIVERSITY LIBRARIES
Mail Code 1103
535 West 114th Street
New York, NY 10027
212-854-2271

Nonprofit Org.
U.S. Postage
PAID
New York, NY
Permit No. 3593

www.columbia.edu/library

the savvy researcher

Improving Your Library Research Skills

Are you struggling with your research? Having trouble figuring out how to locate books? Peer reviewed articles? We'll go over how to locate items in the library system, including how to find online resources through library databases and when to use Interlibrary Loan. Bring your research paper with you -- time will be set aside to answer individual questions.

Drowning in Data? RefWorks can Help

Learn how to use RefWorks, a citation management software program subscribed to by the University of Illinois Library and CITES that is free to faculty, staff, and students of the University of Illinois. This workshop will cover the basics: how to access RefWorks, search catalogs, import references from library databases, retrieve and manage citations, create bibliographies according to various citation styles (e.g., MLA or APA), and use Write N Cite to add parenthetical references to your work. For more information about RefWorks see: http://www.library.uiuc.edu/refworks/

Tools to Stay Current in Your Research

Save valuable research time! Online research resources are pervasive today, making it much harder to stay current in your field. This workshop will introduce several current awareness features including how to set up an RSS feed reader account, creating search alerts from library databases as well as Table of Contents alerts in your discipline.

How To Be A Better RA/TA

Geared towards Research and Teaching Assistants, this library workshop will introduce several time-saving tips. Topics include the basics of working for others (e.g., proxy authorizations and departmental charge accounts), current awareness services, Papersinvited, how to locate dissertations, and how to use RefWorks, a personal citation database.

Citation Chasing: The Grad Student's Guide to the Lit Review

Are you sure you found everything for your lit review? This workshop will cover how to find the tough stuff e.g. conference proceedings, dissertations and statistics. Bring your problem citations, we'll sleuth them out!

Where's the Money? Finding and Securing Grant Funding

Are you trying to find grant funding for a fellowship or scholarship? A research project? We can help you find private and federal funding by searching and setting up alerts in the the Illinois Researcher Information Service, IRIS. We'll also cover the top ten tips of how NOT to get your funding approved.

InfoHacks

Is your academic pile of information overwhelming? Are you looking for new ways to get organized? Learn from the best! Librarians will give you the low-down on how they organize their own research materials using several different strategies including the GTD method (Getting Things Done), citation management, current awareness tools, social bookmarking and quick tips.

Past Writer's Block

Working on a thesis, dissertation, or other lengthy research project? You're not alone! This workshop provides support and helpful tips for doing your research and staying organized as you complete your project.

A Library Introduction to GIS

Curious about how Geographic Information Science (GIS) can enhance your research? Learn about GIS data types like tabular, vector, raster, and geodatabases; and GIS tools such as buffering, overlays, spatial analysis, geocoding, and modeling. GIS is one of the fasting growing research methodologies employed in the sciences, social sciences, and humanities.

Your Research Rights: Ownership Awareness to Maximize the Impact

You're ready to submit your paper for publication. Don't just give over copyright ownership to the publishers. Come to this session and learn how to modify publishers' copyright agreements to suit your future needs. Learn how to make your article free for the whole world to read by putting a copy of it in the university archive, IDEALS. Learn about open access journals - should you publish in one?

Practical Copyright: Considerations for Teaching and Research

You're writing a thesis or preparing to teach your course, but you have a lot of concerns about being ethical and abiding by copyright law. Come to this session and learn the basics of copyright law and some guidelines for how you can stay within the law using the four principles of Fair Use.

4 out of 5 Professors Agree: Citing Polls in Your Papers Will Earn You a Better Grade

Would you like to enhance your research papers with data from public opinion polls? Learn to use the fabulous Roper iPOLL database which contains nearly half a million public opinion survey questions dating (1935 to 2008). Examples using election year topics. No knowledge of statistics or statistical programming is required. The University Library & ATLAS.

Rock the Data, Rock the Vote: Finding and Using National Election Survey Data

The American National Election Studies (ANES) are a series of national surveys of the American electorate taken in every election year since 1948. Create your own tables from the 1948-2004 ANES cumulative file using an online web-based tool. No knowledge of statistics or statistical programming is required. The University Library & ATLAS.

Health, Economic, Social & Political Data for Secondary Analysis

The Inter-university Consortium for Political and Social Research (ICPSR) is the world's largest archive of digital social science data. Learn to search ICPSR's catalog of holdings, download data, and read it into a statistics program (SPSS) to make tables. Our examples will focus on topics suggested by the audience. Some prior experience with SPSS may be helpful, but is not necessary. The University Library & ATLAS.

For dates and times: http://www.library.uiuc.edu/learn/instruction/workshops.html

LEARN
Basics
Research
Instruction
Library Video Network
Workshop Calendar
Send to a Friend
Your Feedback

Undergrads
Graduate Students
Faculty
ESL Students
Alumni
Visitors
Affiliates
Users with Disabilities
Distance Learners
Library Staff
About Us
Site Map

Library » Learn » Instruction » Workshops at the Library

Workshops at the Library

NEW: ONLINE WORKSHOP ON REFWORKS

The Savvy Researcher: Fall 2008 Schedule

ALL WORKSHOPS ARE FREE AND WILL BE HELD IN THE UNDERGRADUATE LIBRARY ROOM 291, **UNLESS OTHERWISE NOTED.**

Drowning in Data? RefWorks can Help

Learn how to use RefWorks, a citation management software program subscribed to by the University of Illinois Library that is free to faculty, staff, and students of the University of Illinois. This workshop will cover the basics: how to access RefWorks, search catalogs, import references from library databases, retrieve and manage citations, create bibliographies according to various citation styles (e.g., MLA or APA), and use Write N Cite to add parenthetical references to your work. For more information about RefWorks see: http://www.library.uiuc.edu/refworks/

Just a few spots left in our last session of the semester!

Registration required: Friday, November 14th 1-2pm

Where's the Money? Finding and Securing Grant Funding

Are you trying to find grant funding for a fellowship or scholarship? A research project? We can help you find private and federal funding by searching and setting up alerts in the the Illinois Researcher Information Service, IRIS. We'll also cover the top ten tips of how NOT to get your funding approved. **Please register by clicking on your date preference.**

Will be rescheduled before the end of the fall semester 2008.

ONLINE WORKSHOP:
Drowning in Data? RefWorks can Help

In this online workshop, learn how to use RefWorks, a citation management software program subscribed to by the University of Illinois Library that is free to faculty, staff, and students of the University of Illinois. This workshop will cover the basics: how to access RefWorks, search catalogs, import references from library databases, retrieve and manage citations, and create bibliographies according to various citation styles (e.g., MLA or APA). For more information about RefWorks see: http://www.library.uiuc.edu/refworks/

Date: November 20, 2008
Time: 6:00-7:00 p.m. CST
Location: Dimdim Meeting Room

Registration is required

This workshop will take place online using Dimdim, a web meeting program. You **must** RSVP to receive a URL and meeting invitation key, which you will receive via email to your illinois.edu account the day prior to the session. Minimum technology requirements to participate:

• Browser: Firefox, Safari or Internet Explorer
• Adobe flash player 9.0 (free download at http://www.adobe.com/products/flashplayer/)

Do you have an idea for a workshop? Contact us!
Missed a workshop? Print the handout!
>> **Do you have a** suggestion for a workshop?

The SRU (for undergraduates)

Citation Tools Workshop
Wednesday, December 3rd, 6:00-7:00pm

Location: Undergraduate Library 291
Audience: Undergraduate students

Registration Information

This workshop will introduce you to citation tools within research databases that you can use to quickly create citations. Citing your sources is a guaranteed way to avoid plagiarism! After this workshop you will be able to easily identify built-in citation tools. Can't attend? Check out our online support.

Requesting Course-Integrated Instruction

Instructional Services

We are here to help you teach! Request assistance in designing and testing library assignments, using library resources in the classroom, and creating class-related bibliographies. You can schedule instructional sessions that are designed specifically for your class, covering areas such as library research strategies, critical thinking skills, and information literacy.

• Contact your departmental library for details on what instructional services they provide or contact Lisa Janicke Hinchliffe, Coordinator for Information Literacy Services and Instruction.
• If you would like instruction for *graduate level ESL classes, the Savvy Researcher Series or other personalized sessions,* please contact Merinda Hensley.
• If you would like instruction for a course that fulfills the *Composition I requirement or Speech Communications 101 or ESL 100 level classes,* please request this instruction through the Undergraduate Library. Information and a request form is available on the Information for Instructors and Faculty page.
• Central Reference helps users of the University Libraries gain the necessary skills for locating and evaluating information through research guides, course-integrated instruction, and individual consultation at the Information Services Desk.

University Library
University of Illinois at Urbana-Champaign
1408 W. Gregory Dr. | Urbana, IL 61801
217-333-2290

For comments on this page contact: Learnlib

Last modified by: Merinda Hensley on 11/13/08

Welcome to the McGill Library

Welcome to McGill University, and welcome to the Library! The Library provides the comprehensive information infrastructure underpinning teaching, learning and research at McGill. Our motto- Information, Innovation, Service - demonstrates commitment to high quality, client-centred information products, services and programs.

The Library consists of 13 branches, primarily disciplinary in focus, located across the University's downtown and Macdonald campuses. Our holdings-- numbering over six million items and including 2.5 million print volumes, over a million e-books and almost 40 000 e-journals-- constitute one of the largest research collections in Canada and the largest in Quebec.

Targeted services connect graduates to the information they need and nurture effective information discovery and use. The Library's attractive facilities-- from pods for group learning to quiet, light-filled study areas, well-equipped e-classrooms and specialized facilities for graduates-- reflect diverse user needs and preferences and encourage positive academic outcomes. Our friendly, knowledgeable staff are always nearby to help with any inquiries.

I invite you to discover all the resources and services the Library offers McGill graduate students. Please let us know any ideas you might have about how we could serve you better.

Janine Schmidt
Trenholme Director of Libraries

2

Getting Started

Begin with the website

The Library's website **www.mcgill.ca/library/** is central to understanding the services available and accessing the resources held. Visit the website and discover a wealth of information; from online databases, statistics, and electronic reference tools, to requesting interlibrary loans and training program details.

Try our subject guides to get started on your research topic

Compiled and maintained by subject-specialist liaison librarians, subject guides provide links to electronic article indexes and databases, lists of relevant print material, and useful websites. Topics covered range from aboriginal health to World War I. Visit **www.mcgill.ca/library-assistance/subject** for the full list of what is available.

Finding journal articles

There are hundreds of **article indexes and databases** that link directly to the online journals to which we subscribe. Some are general in their subject coverage --*Web of Knowledge, Scopus, Academic Search Premier* and *Expanded Academic ASAP* cover all disciplinary areas. Others focus on specific subjects ranging from art history to zoology. These databases help you identify relevant journal articles and other materials related to your topic. Many also provide access to conference proceedings, theses, and other resources. To access our indexes and databases go to **http://mclink.library.mcgill.ca:8331**. They are grouped by broad subject areas and specialized software allows you to search several databases simultaneously.

Finding books and specific journals

The library catalogue contains information on all materials -- print and online-- held by the Library. Searching by author, title, topic, or journal title you can find an item's call number and location as well as the number of copies available, whether material is out on loan and when it is due back. All e-resource records listed in the catalogue contain a web link, and if you use sources like *Google Scholar* you will find some direct links to our catalogue or resources held **(http://catalogue. mcgill.ca)**.

Locating theses and dissertations

Locate existing dissertations in your field by using the following resources:

• To find a McGill thesis, search the library catalogue using the McGill Theses Sub-Catalogue, **http://catalogue.mcgill.ca.**

• *eScholarship@McGill* contains the full text of a growing number of McGill theses lodged in electronic versions **(www.mcgill.ca/library-findinfo/escholarship/).**

• *(Proquest Dissertations & Theses)* Full-text database **(www.mcgill.ca/library-findinfo/ref/s-z/theses/)** includes full-text of over 100,000 dissertations and theses from hundreds of institutions written from 1997 onwards as well as citations and abstracts for many more.

• Theses Canada Portal provides access to the National Library and Archives collection of Canadian theses and dissertations. Full text is available for those published from 1998-2002 **(www.collectionscanada.ca/thesescanada).**

• Index to Theses provides a listing of theses with abstracts (no full text) accepted for higher degrees by universities in Great Britain and Ireland since 1716 **(www.collectionscanada.gc.ca/thesescanada/index-e.html)**

• Online Reference Guide to Theses **(www.library.mcgill.ca/library-findinfo/ref/s-z/theses)** provides links to the above resources and many more.

Digging Deeper

Looking for statistics or needing help analyzing data?

The Electronic Data Resources Service (EDRS) located in Redpath Library Building beside the Loans Desk, provides access to major statistical software programs and has data specialists who can help you find and analyze data relevant to your research. For details, visit the EDRS web page **www.mcgill.ca/edrs/**.

Keeping up to date

Too busy to read all the journals on your topic? The solution is a mere click away! Many journal publishers now offer table of contents alerts in RSS format which can update you in your chosen sphere of interest. Most links are available from the individual journal home page, and some offer groups of journals as a single feed. Databases such as *Academic Search Premier, Applied Science and Technology, Art Retrospective, International Political Science Abstracts, MedLine, Scopus* and many others enable you to save searches and receive updated results in RSS or via email.

Sharing knowledge

The Library is committed to maximizing the research impact of the McGill community and supporting the principles of the scholarly open-access movement. Online submission of theses is made possible through *eScholarship@McGill* **(www.mcgill.ca/library-findinfo/escholarship)** which is a digital repository storing and showcasing the publications and theses of McGill University faculty and students. Submission guidelines, including how to convert your thesis to PDF/A format, can be found on the *eScholarship@McGill* page.

Presenting your findings

Use our online reference listings
www.mcgill.ca/library-findinfo/ref/c-d/conferences/ to
find a conference which might be of interest.

There are also many journals in which you can publish.
Open access journals make content available free. You can
find a list of open-access journals in your field in the
Directory of Open Access Journals at **www.doaj.org/**.
Otherwise try to publish in a journal that allows open
access self-archiving. Search journal policies in the SHER-
PA/RoMEO database at **www.sherpa.ac.uk/romeo.php**.

Make sure you secure your rights as the author when publishing. Use the Creative Commons license
http://creativecommons.org/license/ or the SPARC
Canadian Author Addendum
www.carl-abrc.ca/projects/author/author-e.html.

Do remember to lodge a copy of your paper through
eScholarship@McGill at **www.mcgill.ca/library-
findinfo/escholarship**.

Seeking Assistance

Need help?

Most subject areas have designated liaison librarians who
can assist with your research. Visit
www.mcgill.ca/library-assistance/askus/liaison to find the
right person and to arrange for a consultation. Assistance is
also available:

• in person or over the phone at any one of our branch
libraries. For borrower information, fines, library notices
and PINS, call the Loans Desk
www.mcgill.ca/library-assistance/askus/loansdesks; for
help finding information and assistance with databases or
the library catalogue try
www.mcgill.ca/library-assistance/askus/infodesks/.

- via the website: **www.mcgill.ca/library-using/branches/** for contacts, locations, and opening hours.

- by email at **www.mcgill.ca/library-assistance/askus/email/**.

- through online chat at **www.mcgill.ca/library-assistance/askus/chat/**.

- from a friendly avatar in Second Life **http://slurl.com/secondlife/Cybrary%20City/214/122/24.**

More targeted help in a tour or a class

Want to take a guided tour of one of our branches? Learn how to use specific library resources? Improve your database searching skills? Come to one of our workshops! Further information and a list of upcoming sessions are available at **www.mcgill.ca/library-assistance/classes/**.

Assistance with teaching

If you have teaching commitments, your liaison librarian will prepare and present a library research session tailored for your class. We can help you find online teaching materials and assist you in creating links from your course reading lists into our online holdings

(**www.mcgill.ca/library-support/teaching**). These can easily be integrated into *myCourses* (WebCT Vista) so that your students can directly access electronic material owned at McGill.

Library Matters

Accessing your library account

Your library account contains information on your current loans, loan history and hold requests. To access, go to the library catalogue at **http://catalogue.mcgill.ca**, click on the SIGN IN box in the upper right hand corner, and sign in using your McGill ID card barcode and your PIN. Your default PIN is your birth date in the form yyyymmdd, which you may change any time. Once you are signed in you can check your account, renew current loans, and place hold requests for items on loan to other users.

Borrowing an item from McGill

Borrow books and other items by bringing them to the loans desk or by using one of the auto-loan machines located in each of our branches. As a graduate student, you may borrow regular loan items for 6 weeks at a time and you may renew them twice; however, items may be recalled if needed for course reserve or if they are requested by another user. It is important for you to keep track of your library account by signing in regularly to the catalogue or by checking your McGill email address as this is how we will notify you of recalls and overdue items.

If you are on the downtown campus and need something from the Macdonald Campus Library (or vice-versa), you can fill out a request online at **www.mcgill.ca/library-using/mcgillloans/intercampus** and we will deliver the item for you.

If McGill does not have what you are looking for.

We can buy books you might need for your research. You can send an email to your liaison librarian or make a suggestion online at **www.mcgill.ca/library/assistance/askus/suggest/**.

You may also obtain materials from CISTI Source, which is an electronic direct ordering service from CISTI (Canadian Institute for Scientific and Technical Information). Use this service first to request journal articles and conference papers not held by the Library. Each department has a user name and password for ordering documents which you can obtain from your Departmental Representative. Visit **www.library.mcgill.ca/psel/pseill/cisti/swetscan.htm**.

Alternatively you can borrow books directly from other university libraries. You may obtain a reciprocal borrowing card issued under an agreement with CREPUQ (Conférence des Recteurs et des Principaux des Universités du Québec). This card allows you to borrow at participating Canadian university libraries, subject to restrictions determined by individual libraries (a list of participating libraries is available at **www.cop-pul.ca/rb/rblibs.html**). To obtain a CREPUQ card, bring your valid McGill ID to the Office of the Director of Libraries on the entry floor of McLennan Library Building.

You can use McGill's Interlibrary Loans Service to locate books that are not owned by any McGill library and articles and conference papers not available from CISTI Source. Response time varies from 2 days to 3 weeks depending on the requested material and the supplier. Make your requests using COLOMBO at **www.mcgill.ca/library-using/otherloans/colombo**. For graduate students using the Life Sciences Library, visit **www.mcgill.ca/lsl/services/ill/**.

You are also entitled to borrow materials on a long-term basis from CRL, the Center for Research Libraries. For more information on CRL collections, check **www.crl.edu/**. You can search for and request CRL materials through COLOMBO as already described.

Using Library resources away from campus

If you plan to do research while at home or on the road, get connected to the network with McGill's Dialup Access Service (DAS) or through the Virtual Private Network (VPN). If you do not have a commercial Internet service provider (ISP) you can connect via McGill's DAS service. To find out how, go to **www.mcgill.ca/ics/tools/das**. If you connect to the Internet with a commercial ISP (e.g. *Videotron, Bell Sympatico*) you can link up via McGill's VPN service. To set up the VPN on your computer go to **www.mcgill.ca/ics/tools/vpn**.

Acknowledging your sources: plagiarism and academic integrity

Remember that when you use someone else's words or ideas, you must acknowledge the original source. Keep track of information sources when researching in order to cite them properly. For guides on how to cite items appropriately, visit **www.mcgill.ca/library-assistance/how-to/citing**.

Citing your sources

Citation management software allows you to create and organize reference lists and bibliographies for your research. When searching library catalogues and databases you may export references directly into your personal database or save them as text files and import them. You may output your reference lists in almost any citation style. The Library has purchased a university-wide site license for *EndNote* and *Reference Manager*, and offers training in using both programs. Download these programs free of charge to your office, laptop or home computer. You will find more information, schedules for upcoming training sessions and downloading instructions at **www.mcgill.ca/library-using/computers/endnote**.

10

Protecting everyone's rights

The Library aims to protect the rights of the McGill community to use electronic resources for their educational, scholarly, teaching and research purposes, while at the same time protecting the right of copyright holders from unauthorized reproduction of their works. No copyrighted work may be copied, published, disseminated, displayed, performed or played without permission of the copyright holder except when it is within the limitations of fair dealing as provided by the law. For more details, please refer to **www.mcgill.ca/library-assistance/copyright**.

Too much of a good thing

Excessive downloading of articles jeopardizes the University's access to electronic resources. Students are permitted to download, save, print and store single copies of individual articles for educational and research purposes only. Students are not permitted to print out entire issues of online journals, multiple copies of a particular article or large sections from electronic books. For more information please consult **www.mcgill.ca/library-using/policies/licensing**.

Spaces For You

Each library has computers, printers, photocopiers, and facilities for plugging in laptops and connecting to the University's wireless network. Refurbished spaces in most branch libraries provide attractive spaces conductive to individual study and group learning.

Opening hours vary for each library. Most are open up to 90 hours per week with extended opening hours around examination time, including 24-hr opening for the Humanities and Social Sciences Library. More information about facilities can be found at the branch library webpages: **www.mcgill.ca/library-using/branches/**.

After-hours access

Graduate students may access the Nahum Gelber Law and Schulich Science and Engineering Libraries when the libraries are closed. Access is usually restricted to graduate students and staff in the departments served by the individual branch library. Contact your branch for more information.

Special facilities targeted for graduate student use

Several branch libraries have specialized facilities for graduate students. They comprise individual study desks, fitted with side partitions and a shelf or drawer in which books may be kept during the session. Graduates who are currently writing theses and do not have office space may book small rooms or desks in some libraries. Graduate facilities are available in the Humanities and Social Sciences Library, Education Library and Curriculum Resources Centre, Macdonald Campus Library, Nahum Gelber Law Library, Marvin Duchow Music Library and the Schulich Library of Science and Engineering.

Getting together in groups

The new Cyberthèque in the Humanities and Social Sciences Library provides glass-encased group study pods which may be booked at the Information Desk and booth-like banquettes  which can be utilized for group work. Several private study rooms are available in the Humanities and Social Sciences Library for the use of current graduate students. Each study room is shared by two students and sharing arrangements are the responsibility of the paired students. More information is available at **www.library.mcgill.ca/hssl/facilities/study.** Group study facilities are available for booking in most branch libraries.

Users with disabilities

McGill Library and the Office for Students with Disabilities coordinate programs and services with the goal of providing a rewarding library experience to users with disabilities. The Office for Students with Disabilities runs a small computer lab staffed by an adaptive technologist in Room 5B on the entry floor of the Redpath Library Building. McGill Library also offers library instruction on demand for students with hearing, learning, and visual disabilities. For more information visit **www.mcgill.ca/library-support/disabilities/**

Maps

Downtown campus

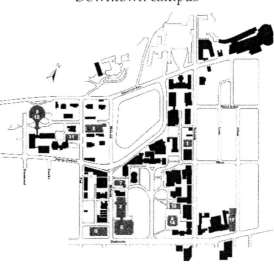

1. Birks Reading Room

2. Blackader-Lauterman Library of Architecture and Art

3. Education Library and Curriculum Resources Centre

4. Edward Rosenthall Mathematics and Statistics Library

5. Howard Ross Library of Management

6. Humanities and Social Sciences Library

6. Rare Books & Special Collections

7. Islamic Studies Library

8. Life Sciences Library

9. Macdonald Campus Library

10. Marvin Duchow Music Library

11. Nahum Gelber Law Library

12. Osler Library of the History of Medicine

13. Schulich Library of Science and Engineering

14. Walter Hitschfeld Geographic Information Centre

Macdonald campus

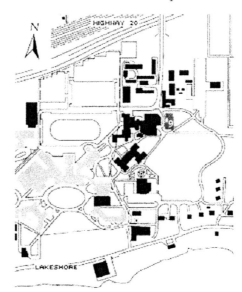

Contact Us

Branch libraries

Birks Reading Room
William and Henry Birks Bldg.
514-398-4127
www.mcgill.ca/birks/

Blackader-Lauterman Library
of Architecture and Art
McLennan-Redpath Library Bldg.
514-398-4743
www.mcgill.ca/blackader/

Education Library and Curriculum
Resources Centre
Education Bldg.
514-398-4686
www.mcgill.ca/education-library/

Edward Rosenthall Mathematics
and Statistics Library
Burnside Hall, 11th Floor
514-398-4676
www.mcgill.ca/rosenthall/

Electronic Data Resource Service
(EDRS)
McLennan-Redpath Library Bldg.
514-398-1429
www.mcgill.ca/edrs/

Howard Ross Management Library
Bronfman Bldg., 2nd Floor
514-398-4690
www.mcgill.ca/howardross/

Humanities and Social Sciences
Library
McLennan-Redpath Library Bldg.
514-398-4734
www.mcgill.ca/hssl/

Islamic Studies Library
Morrice Hall
514-398-4685
www.mcgill.ca/islamic-library/

Life Sciences Library
McIntyre Medical Sciences Bldg.,
3rd Floor
514-398-4475
www.mcgill.ca/lsl/

Macdonald Campus Library
Barton Bldg., Macdonald Campus
Ste. Anne de Bellevue
514-398-7881
www.mcgill.ca/macdonald-library/

Marvin Duchow Music Library
New Music Bldg., 3rd Floor
514-398-4695
www.mcgill.ca/music-library/

Nahum Gelber Law Library
514-398-4715
www.mcgill.ca/law-library/

Osler Library (History of Medicine)
McIntyre Medical Sciences Bldg.,
3rd Floor
514-398-4475 x09873
www.mcgill.ca/osler-library/

Rare Books & Special Collections
McLennan-Redpath Library Bldg,
4th Floor.
514-398-4711
www.mcgill.ca/rarebooks/

Schulich Library of Science
and Engineering
Macdonald-Stewart Library Bldg.
514-398-4769
www.mcgill.ca/schulich/

Walter Hitschfeld Geographic
Information Centre
Burnside Hall, 5th Floor
514-398-8095
www.mcgill.ca/gic/

Office of the Director of Libraries

McLennan-Redpath Library Bldg.
3459 McTavish
Montreal, QC H3A 1Y1
Tel: 514-398-4677
Fax: 514-398-7356
Email: doadmin.library@mcgill.ca
Web: www.mcgill.ca/library/

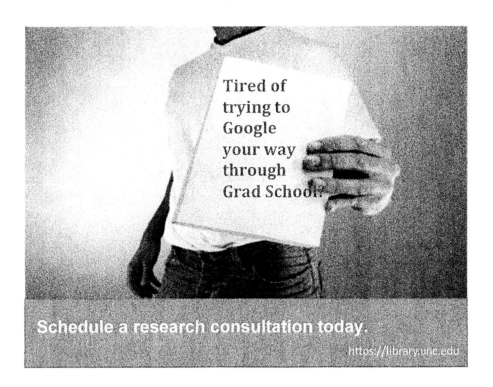

*Teaching for
the first time?*

*Learn how
the   library can help.*

✓ Reserve readings

✓ Customized Blackboard course pages

✓ Instruction sessions tailored to your assignments

To learn more, go to http://library.unc.edu

Not sure how to start that lit review?   We can help.

 UNC
UNIVERSITY LIBRARY

http://library.unc.edu

Faculty Commons Spring Quarter 2008 Calendar

301 Alden Library

PHOTOS BY WILLIAM DINKLEY

For a complete schedule of events visit www.library.ohiou.edu/fc/

APRIL 2008

LIBRARY WORKSHOP: ORIENTATION ON FACULTY COMMONS RESOURCES

Friday, April 11, 2008 | Facilitated by Faculty Commons Directors and Staff
1:00 - 2:00 PM | 301U Faculty Commons
This one hour workshop will provide information about faculty development programs and resources available through the four Centers within the Faculty Commons, including collaborative faculty development initiatives. (co-sponsored with Alden Library's workshop series)
www.library.ohiou.edu/fc • 740.597.1777 • facultycommons@ohio.edu

ENHANCING TEACHING AND LEARNING WITH PODCASTS (CAT)

Tuesday, April 15, 2008 | 11:15 AM - 12:00 N
Wednesday, April 16, 2008 | 4:00 - 4:45 PM
301U Faculty Commons | Facilitated by Kate Anderson, Media Production
Podcasts allow teachers and students to create and share knowledge via voice recordings, sound effects, photos, and movies. This workshop offers an introduction to podcasting: what it is, how to use it to enhance teaching and learning, and how to create and deliver podcasts with easy-to-use audio recording and editing software such as Audacity and iMovie.
www.citl.ohiou.edu • 740.593.2280 • andersk8@ohio.edu

THE FACULTY COMMONS & ALDEN LIBRARY LUNCHBAG SERIES EXPLORING THE RESEARCH PROCESS: *From first draft to production, the making of Knock Me A Kiss*

Wednesday, April 16, 2008 | Presenter Charles Smith, Professor of Playwriting Program, School of Theater
12:00 N | Friends of the Libraries Room
A new monthly series co-sponsored with Alden Library. Experience the ways in which OU faculty creatively use library resources, while they share their most recent discoveries.
www.library.ohiou.edu/workshops/ • 740.597.1238 • wochna@ohio.edu

APPALACHIAN LEARNING COMMUNITY (SLC): *Honorable Soldiers Too: An historical case study of post-reconstruction African-American female teachers of the upper Ohio valley*

Thursday, April 17, 2008 | Presenter: Carole Wylie Hancock, Professor, Washington State Community College
6:30 PM | 301U Faculty Commons
A fascinating and rich study documenting the experiences of six women who lived in Athens, Parkersburg, and Monongahela City, PA. Come enjoy the history you don't know about Appalachia - black schools and teachers. Lots of photos. Open to the public.
http://appalachia.citl.ohiou.edu/index.html • 740.593.2546 • graybill@ohio.edu

WORKSHOP SERIES (CTL / CAT / CWE): *Getting Ready for Learning Outcomes in Tier 1 Courses*

Thursday and Friday, April 17 & 18, May 1 & 2, and May 22 & 23, 2008 | Facilitated by Laurie Hatch, Director of CTL and Professor of Sociology
1:00 - 3:00 PM | 301U Faculty Commons
This three-part workshop series will provide informational materials, collegial sharing of ideas, and hands-on assistance for faculty and instructional staff who are incorporating learning outcomes in their Tier 1 courses. For the three workshops in this series, please *RSVP for* either the Thursday or Friday meeting days. (The same workshop topic will be addressed during that week. Up to 10 participants can be accommodated in the Thursday workshops and up to 10 in the Friday workshops. A stipend will be offered to participants; see reverse for details.)
Please RSVP to facultycommons@ohio.edu
www.ohiou.edu/ctl • 740.593.2681 • ctl@ohio.edu

TEACHING PORTFOLIOS FOR FUTURE FACULTY (CTL)

Tuesday, April 22; May 6; & May 20, 2008 | Facilitated by Tim Vickers, Associate Director of CTL
10:00 AM - 12:00 N | 301U Faculty Commons
A three-part workshop series for graduate students on the professional teaching portfolio and the critical role it can play in securing a faculty position and achieving success in the professoriate.
www.ohiou.edu/ctl • 740.593.2681 • ctl@ohio.edu

TURNING SCIENCE STUDENTS INTO SCIENCE WRITERS (CWE)

Wednesday, April 23, 2008 | Facilitated by Sarah Wyatt, Associate Professor of Environmental and Plant Biology, and Sherrie Gradin, Director of CWE and Professor of English
1:00 - 5:00 PM | 301U Faculty Commons | Refreshments will be served
This seminar focuses on strategies to help students better understand and implement scientific writing conventions. The conversation will include ideas for integrating aspects of science writing into daily assignments, class discussions, and exam questions. Strategies for perfecting formal science writing assignments such as lab reports and literature reviews ("research papers") will also be discussed.
www.ohiou.edu/writing • 740.597.1869 • wac@ohio.edu

CREATING E-PORTFOLIOS WITH WORDPRESS (CAT)

Thursday, April 24, 2008 | Instructor Paul O'Donnell, CAT
1:00 - 3:00 PM | 301U Faculty Commons
Electronic portfolios showcase your academic accomplishments. This hands-on workshop will help you register a Wordpress account, create and edit pages, add multimedia, and customize your portfolio's appearance. Bring only a flash drive or disk containing your digital artifacts and, if you have one, a laptop.
www.citl.ohiou.edu • 740.597.2706 • odonnelp@ohio.edu

TIPS FOR FACULTY RESEARCH AND PUBLISHING (CTL)

Friday, April 25, 2008 | Facilitated by Laurie Hatch, Director of CTL and Professor of Sociology
12:00 N - 1:00 PM | Southern Campus
This session will feature a mini-presentation and discussion of faculty research and publishing tips, focusing particularly on the scholarship of teaching and learning.
www.ohiou.edu/ctl • 740.593.2681 • ctl@ohio.edu

USING CLICKERS TO PROMOTE STUDENT ENGAGEMENT (CAT)

Wednesday, April 30, 2008 | Instructor Mike Roy, CAT
1:00 - 3:00 PM | 301U Faculty Commons
Clickers are hand-held devices that allow all students--not just a vocal minority-- to answer the instructor's questions. Attend this workshop to learn how you can use clickers to gauge student comprehension, respond to misconceptions, address ambiguities, generate dialogue, open new avenues of discussion, and otherwise engage the class.
www.citl.ohiou.edu/clickers • 740.597.2706 • roy@ohio.edu

MAY 2008

WORKSHOP SERIES (CTL / CAT / CWE): *Getting Ready for Learning Outcomes in Tier 1 Courses*

Thursday and Friday, May 1 & 2, and May 22 & 23, 2008 | Facilitated by Laurie Hatch, Director of CTL and Professor of Sociology
1:00 - 3:00 PM | 301U Faculty Commons
Second in a three-part workshop series: see April 17 & 18 for complete workshop description.
www.ohiou.edu/ctl • 740.593.2681 • ctl@ohio.edu

TEACHING PORTFOLIOS FOR FUTURE FACULTY (CTL)

Tuesday, May 6 & May 20, 2008 | Facilitated by Tim Vickers, Associate Director of CTL
10:00 AM - 12:00 N | 301U Faculty Commons
Second of a three-part workshop series for graduate students: see April 22 listing for complete workshop details.
www.ohiou.edu/ctl • 740.593.2681 • ctl@ohio.edu

TIPS FOR FACULTY RESEARCH AND PUBLISHING (CTL)

Friday, May 7, 2008 | Facilitated by Laurie Hatch, Director of CTL and Professor of Sociology
1:00 - 2:30 PM | Chillicothe Campus, Room 110 Bennett Hall
This session will feature a mini-presentation and discussion of faculty research and publishing tips, focusing particularly on the scholarship of teaching and learning.
www.ohiou.edu/ctl • 740.593.2681 • ctl@ohio.edu

TEACHING WRITING IN THE DISCIPLINES (CWE)

Friday, May 9, 2008 | Facilitated by Sherrie Gradin, Director of CWE and Professor of English and Melanie Lee, Assistant Director of CWE
1:00 - 4:00 PM | 301U Faculty Commons | Refreshments will be served
This seminar will address writing for both major-area students, who need to learn the conventions and styles of the discipline, as well as for student writers in courses from a variety of fields. Teaching Writing in the Disciplines provides faculty with information and support for working with their students' writing. We will discuss what we expect from our students, how we might write better assignments to encourage those expectations, and strategies other instructors use to teach writing in various disciplines.
www.ohiou.edu/writing • 740.597.1869 • wac@ohio.edu

NEGOTIATING PLAGIARISM: DEFINITIONS AND RESPONSES (CWE)

Monday, May 12, 2008 | Facilitated by Sherrie Gradin, Director of CWE and Professor of English
1:00 - 5:00 PM | 301U Faculty Commons | Refreshments will be served
Plagiarism is a problem for all institutions of higher learning. Horror stories of cheating—buying papers, handing in a roommate's paper, cutting and pasting from the Internet, lifting material from other texts without citation or quotation—abound. As we struggle with our own responses of anger, frustration, and even betrayal, we ask why and how plagiarism got to be so rampant and what we can do to restore academic integrity to our campuses. In this seminar, our discussion will be grounded in research on plagiarism and the scholarship of textual borrowing. We will examine definitions of plagiarism, a range of appropriate responses, and then discuss actions we can take as teachers and mentors to create learning environments where student plagiarism is less likely to occur.
www.ohiou.edu/writing • 740.597.1869 • wac@ohio.edu

THE FACULTY COMMONS & ALDEN LIBRARY LUNCHBAG SERIES EXPLORING THE RESEARCH PROCESS: *Sex, Drugs & Rock 'n Roll: Researching Counterculture in Latin America*

Thursday May 15, 2008 | Presenter Patrick Barr-Melej, Associate Professor, History/Latin American Studies
12:00 N | Friends of the Libraries Rooms
A new monthly series co-sponsored with Alden Library. Experience the ways in which OU faculty creatively use library resources, while they share their most recent discoveries.
www.library.ohiou.edu/workshops/ • 740.597.1238 • wochna@ohio.edu

BLOGS, WIKIS, AND MEETING STUDENTS WHERE THEY WRITE (CWE)

Friday, May 16, 2008 | Facilitated by Sherrie Gradin, Director of CWE and Professor of English, and Paul Shovlin, Assistant Director of CWE
10:00 AM - 2:00 PM | 301U Faculty Commons
Our special emphasis in this seminar will be on using blogs and wikis as a means of writing and writing to learn. Faculty will exchange their views regarding these technologies and how we might use them in the classroom. Since we will have a mix of skill levels, we will cover the basics for those less experienced. We will learn how to create and manage our own blogs and wikis for course use and see examples of the ways these tools can enhance students' learning.
www.ohiou.edu/writing • 740.597.1869 • wac@ohio.edu

TEACHING PORTFOLIOS FOR FUTURE FACULTY (CTL)

Tuesday, May 20, 2008 | Facilitated by Tim Vickers, Associate Director of CTL
10:00 AM - 12:00 N | 301U Faculty Commons
Third session of a three-part workshop series for graduate students: see April 22 listing for complete workshop details.
www.ohiou.edu/ctl • 740.593.2681 • ctl@ohio.edu

WORKSHOP SERIES (CTL / CAT / CWE): *Getting Ready for Learning Outcomes in Tier 1 Courses*

Thursday and Friday, May 22 & 23, 2008 | Facilitated by Laurie Hatch, Director of CTL and Professor of Sociology
1:00 - 3:00 PM | 301U Faculty Commons
Third in a three-part workshop series: see April 17 & 18 for complete workshop description.
www.ohiou.edu/ctl • 740.593.2681 • ctl@ohio.edu

THE FACULTY COMMONS & ALDEN LIBRARY LUNCHBAG SERIES EXPLORING THE RESEARCH PROCESS: *Case Report: Forensic Investigation of 'the Mystery Stain' at the old Athens Asylum*

Wednesday, May 28, 2008 | Presenter Glen Jackson, Assistant Professor of Chemistry and Biochemistry
12:00 N | Friends of the Libraries Rooms
A new monthly series co-sponsored with Alden Library. Experience the ways in which OU faculty creatively use library resources, while they share their most recent discoveries.
www.library.ohiou.edu/workshops/ • 740.597.1238 • wochna@ohio.edu

JUNE 2008

TEACHING & LEARNING MINI-CONFERENCE (CTL / CWE / CAT / CCE)

Monday, June 16, 2008 | Conference organizers: Laurie Hatch, Director of CTL and Professor of Sociology and Tim Vickers, Associate Director of CTL.
9:00 AM – 3:00 PM | Faculty Commons / Friends of the Libraries Room
This mini-conference will feature sessions on student learning outcomes and assessment; peer mentoring for faculty; and the common reading project. Further details will be available at http://www.ohiou.edu/ctl/

KEY TO SPONSORS:
Center for Academic Technology (CAT)
Campus-Community Engagement (CCE)
Center for Teaching & Learning (CTL)
Center for Writing Excellence (CWE)
Scholarly Learning Community (SLC)

FAQs

What is the FC?
The Faculty Commons is a program for faculty to socialize, study, access and use technology, and attend events. The FC is a large open area where they can attend workshops, access computerized personal time, or room with other faculty. The space is surrounded by well-equipped conference rooms, and the Friends of the Library Room.

Where is the FC?
The Faculty Commons is located on the 2nd floor of Alden Library.

How long is the FC open?
The hours are in a line with our program.

Who can use the FC?
It is open to all Ohio University staff and faculty. To receive a conference room, call the Faculty Commons at 740.597.2772 or email facultycommons@ohio.edu. Please stop in for a visit anytime! All Friends of the Library Room are open to consult the Alden Library administrative office at 740.593.2702.

What offices are located here?
The Faculty Commons houses a range of Community Engagement, the Center for Teaching & Learning, the Center for Writing Excellence, Library Collections and Media Production.

Find These Resources at The Faculty Commons

Where faculty can find support for their teaching, scholarship and engagement as well as a place to relax and share a cup of coffee.

Center for Academic Technology (CAIT). An academic support for faculty interested in educational technology. Faculty day-week presentation on designing, developing and assessing instruction; includes resource materials and technology related tools and resources. www.catl.ohiou.edu

Campus Community Engagement (OCEN). Dedicated to bringing together and resources to university community engagement activities. We collaborate with faculty, staff, departments, colleges and community-based groups. connect@ohiou.edu, www.engagement.ohiou.edu

Center for Teaching and Learning (CTL). Works collaboratively with university colleagues to enhance the connection between teaching and planning. CTL offers workshops, discussion series, individual consultations, and other programs and resources for faculty teaching associates, and instructional staff. Through CTL programs and institutes, colleagues across the university share ideas and perspectives with one another on issues of teaching and learning. www.ohiou.edu/ctl

Center for Writing Excellence (CWE). Collaborates with other faculty development, while on campus and is dedicated to enriching student learning and faculty teaching through writing. The CWE includes Writing Across the Curriculum, the Student Writing Center, and the Ohio University Appalachian Writing Project. www.ohio.edu/writing

Library Collections Development. The Assistant Dean for Collections and Access has overall responsibility for the University's unique collection development activities and budget, and oversees the collection development activities of approximately 25 librarians who serve as subject specialists to the University's academic departments and colleges. www.library.ohiou.edu/info/libcoll/dev

Media Production. Supports multi-disciplinary research presentation with various design and digital project preparation. We prepare both one-phase printing and group learning in a multimedia content design and formatting. Additionally, digital photo services including web scanning, photo retouching, copy/stand work and scan/stand printing slides are available. www.ohiou.edu/mediaproduction

"Smart" Conference Rooms for faculty meetings.
To reserve, call the Faculty Commons at 597.1777 or email facultycommons@ohio.edu

OHIO UNIVERSITY

Office of the Executive
Vice President and Provost

Faculty Commons
Alden 361
Athens OH 45701-2979

FACULTY COMMONS SPRING QUARTER 2008 CALENDAR!

Learning Outcomes at Ohio University and Support for Faculty and Instructional Staff

In March 2007 the Faculty Senate at Ohio University passed a new requirement for all course syllabi:

> "The intended learning outcomes or objectives upon successful completion of the class are to be included in the syllabus."

As noted in a November 2007 letter to Ohio University faculty from David O. Thomas (Chair, University Curriculum Council), Vice-Chair, Faculty Senate) and David C. Ingram (Chair, Educational Programs and Student Affairs, Faculty Senate), "the Faculty Senate's intent of requiring specific learning outcomes on course syllabi is threefold: a) learning outcomes provide students with an understanding of what they are expected to learn from a given course; b) learning outcomes can help others (prospective students, their parents, graduate schools, etc.) understand what our students have learned from a given course or program; and c) clear learning outcomes can assist with curriculum development and program planning."

The University Curriculum Committee anticipates a two-year, phased-in process to incorporate learning outcomes into our curriculum. Beginning Winter Quarter, 2008, all new courses submitted to the University Curriculum Council are to include learning outcomes. By September 2008, learning outcomes should be included for all General Education Tier 1 offerings (see http://www.ohiou.edu/learning/objectives for the learning outcomes suggested by the General Education Outcomes Committee). By the end of Fall 2008, learning outcomes should be included in the syllabi for all courses at Ohio University.

A number of faculty in programs across the university already include student learning outcomes in course syllabi and collect systematic evidence of student learning. These colleagues will be important campus resources as the learning outcomes initiative gets underway.

Support is available through the Center for Teaching & Learning and Faculty Commons for faculty and instructors who are new to learning outcomes and assessment, and/or who will be redesigning their courses to incorporate learning outcomes:

Tier 1 Learning Outcomes Workshop Series. A workshop series focusing on learning outcomes in Tier 1 courses will be offered Spring quarter (see calendar of events on the reverse). Up to 20 workshop participants can be accommodated (10 each in the Thursday and Friday workshop sessions); seats will be filled as RSVP's are received (contact facultycommons@ohio.edu). Stipends of $1,000 are available for faculty and instructors of Tier 1 courses who participate in these learning outcomes workshops and who generate a learning outcomes action plan for a selected course.

Tier 1 courses are the focus of the Spring 2008 workshops since these courses are expected to include learning outcomes by Fall 2008. We anticipate offering similar sets of learning outcomes workshops in Summer 2008 and during the 2008-09 academic year.

Teaching & Learning Mini-Conference (June 16 in the Faculty Commons/Alden Library; see calendar of events on reverse) will include several workshops on learning outcomes and assessment. Faculty at regional campuses who plan to attend: please email facultycommons@ohio.edu to inquire about mileage reimbursement.

Diversity Awareness Month...

Please join your colleagues for an informal discussion and public lecture featuring Ohio University guest speaker Dr. Peggy McIntosh

Peggy McIntosh, Ph.D., the Associate Director of the Wellesley College Center for Research on Women, is the founder and co-director of the National S.E.E.D. (Seeking Educational Equity and Diversity) Project on Inclusive Curriculum. A world-renowned lecturer, she consults with higher education institutions throughout the United States and the world on creating multicultural and gender-fair curricula. Author of many influential articles on curriculum change, women's studies and systems of unearned privilege, she has taught at Harvard University, Trinity College (Washington, DC) and the University of Durham (England), among other institutions.

Informal Discussion: Monday, April 14, 10:00 AM - 12N
Friends of the Libraries Room

Public Lecture: Monday, April 14, 7:30 PM
Baker University Center Ballroom
(admission to the lecture is free and open to the public)

Sponsored by the Provost Office of Diversity, Access, and Equity and the College of Education

Scholarly Learning Community Call for Proposals

The Center for Teaching & Learning and Faculty Commons invite applications for Scholarly Learning Communities to be sponsored Spring quarter 2008. All faculty and instructional staff are cordially invited to apply. For details and the application form, see www.ohiou.edu/ctl. Questions can be directed to Laurie Hatch, Director, CTL, hatchl@ohio.edu, 740.597.2700.

Located in Alden Library, Faculty Commons and library staff provide professional development opportunities for the Ohio University community.

For a complete schedule of Faculty Commons events visit www.library.ohiou.edu/fc/

For a complete list of upcoming Alden Library workshops visit www.library.ohiou.edu/workshops/

You're @ the Library. A guide to using the OSU Libraries.

20 Questions about the Library for Grad Students

Important Library Numbers:

Hours Hotline
405-744-5029

Circulation Desk
405-744-6812

Library Web site
www.library.okstate.edu

Library Catalog
*http://osucatalog.library.
okstate.edu*

*Help accessing online
journals & databases*
405-744-9161
877-744-9161 toll free

1. Where is the Library?

The Edmon Low Library is centrally located. It is north of the Student Union and is the only other building on campus with a bell tower. The Stillwater campus also has four branch libraries: the Architecture Library, in the ATRC; the Mary L. Williams Curriculum Materials Library, in Willard Hall; the North Boomer Annex; and the William E. Brock Memorial Library, in McElroy Hall.

2. What remote services are offered?

You can use the Library's Web site to access the OSU Library Catalog (where you can check the status of material and renew items you have), about 200 electronic databases, more than 37,000 full-text journals, online course reserves and email reference assistance and tech support. To access these tools off-campus you need to logon to the EZProxy. There are detailed instructions at www.library. okstate.edu/dls/ezproxy.htm.

Our Digital Library Services (DLS) Department is available to answer questions about the Library's electronic resources. Contact DLS at 405-744-9161, toll-free 877-744-9161 or via email at lib-dls@okstate.edu.

3. When is the Library open?

During the regular semesters the Main Library is open Mon.-Thu. 7:30 am-2 am, Fri. 7:30 am-9 pm, Sat. 10 am-9 pm and Sun. 10 am-2 am. Hours vary during holidays and intersessions. For the most up to date hours, call 405-744-5029 or visit www. library.okstate.edu/.

4. How many books can I check out?

Graduate students can have 100 books out at a time.

5. How long can I keep books?

Grad students have a loan period of 120 days. There are special materials (videos, DVD's, maps, reserve materials, branch library books) that have shorter loan periods. Staff will tell you when items are due. You may renew most items online.
➥ Register your email at the Circulation Desk and we will send you reminders before your books are due!

6. Can I bring food or drinks to the Library?

Yes, you may bring drinks with a lid and small snack items. The Edmon Low Library even has a cafe where you can buy specialty coffees and snacks.

7. How much are fines?

Standard overdue fines are $.25/day/book. Reserve, re-called and special permission materials have higher fines ranging from $5/day to $1/hour. Un paid fines are billed to your Bursar's account. You may renew most items online.

8. Are there computers I can use in the Library?

Over 100 internet stations are located on the 1st and 5th floors. At these computers you can use MS Office, search and print from the Web, OSU Library Catalog and other library electronic resources.

OSU students can also check out laptops at the Circulation Desk on the 1st floor. Laptops (including your own!) can access the Web anywhere in the building and at least one printer is on each floor.

9. Are there Librarians who specialize in my discipline?

Each academic department has a Subject Specialist Librarian. Most Specialists hold a degree in that subject or a related field. If you would like the Library to purchase material contact your Specialist. A list of the Subject Specialist Librarians can be found at www.library.okstate.edu/services/liaisons.htm.

Contact for information:
Reference Desk
405-744-9775 or
877-744-9161 toll free

You're @ the Library. A guide to using the OSU Libraries.

20 Questions about the Library for Faculty

Important Library Numbers:

Hours Hotline
405-744-5029

Circulation Desk
405-744-6812

Library Website
www.library.okstate.edu

Library Catalog
http://osucatalog.library.
okstate.edu

*Help accessing online
journals & databases*
405-744-9161
877-744-9161 toll free

1. Where is the Library?

The Edmon Low Library is north of the Student Union and also has a bell tower. The Stillwater campus has four branch libraries: the Architecture Library, in the ATRC; the Mary L. Williams Curriculum Materials Library, in Willard Hall; the North Boomer Annex; and the Brock Memorial Library, in McElroy Hall.

2. What remote services are offered?

You can use the Library's Web site to access the OSU Library Catalog (where you can check the status of material and renew items you have), approximately 200 electronic databases, over 37,000 full-text journals and email reference assistance and tech support. To access these tools off-campus you need to log in. There are detailed instructions at www.library.okstate.edu/dls/ezproxy.htm.

Our Digital Library Services (DLS) Department is available to answer questions about the Library's electronic resources. Contact DLS at 405-744-9161, toll-free 877-744-9161 or via email at lib-dls@okstate.edu.

3. When is the Library open?

During the regular semesters the Main Library is open Mon.-Thu. 7:30 am-2 am, Fri. 7:30 am-9 pm, Sat. 10 am-9 pm and Sun. 10 am-2 am. Hours vary during holidays

and intersessions. For the most up to date hours, call 405-744-5029 or visit www.library.okstate.edu/.

4. For how long & how many books can I check out?

Faculty have two due dates a year, February 27 and August 31. There are special materials (laptops, videos, DVD's, maps, branch library books) that have shorter loan periods. Staff will tell you when items are due. You may renew most items online. Faculty can have 150 items checked out.

5. Where can I find reference assistance?

Librarians or Library GAs are available at the Reference Desk on the 1st floor to answer questions and give hands-on instruction 94 hours a week. We offer assistance in person, by phone 405-744-9775, via email lib-dls@okstate.edu or via chat and IM. IM & chat reference is available Mon.-Thu. 1 pm-9 pm & Fri. 1 pm-5 pm. Add our screen name to your contact list in AOL or Yahoo!: OkstateLibrary; ICQ: 195159930; MSN: OkstateLibrary@hotmail.com.

6. Can I find recently purchased books?

Many new books are displayed on the 1st floor north side. You can also search for recent acquisitions in the OSU Library Catalog. Click "Basic" or "Advanced" search from the homepage and select "New Books.

7. Can I place things on reserve?

Yes. The OSU Library offers both hard copy Reserves, at the Circulation Desk on the 1st floor, and electronic Reserves. You can place items on Reserve by completing a Reserve Materials Request Form. The form is available at the Circulation Desk or online at http://reserves.library.okstate.edu/index.htm.

8. Are there Librarians who specialize in my discipline?

Each academic department has a Subject Specialist Librarian. Most hold a degree in that subject or a related field. If you would like the Library to purchase material contact your Specialist. A list of the Subject Specialist Librarians can be found at www.library.okstate.edu/services/liaisons.htm.

Your Specialist can also give you information on our resources and services or give library instruction to your students.

Contact for information:
Reference Desk
405-744-9775 or
877-744-9161 toll free

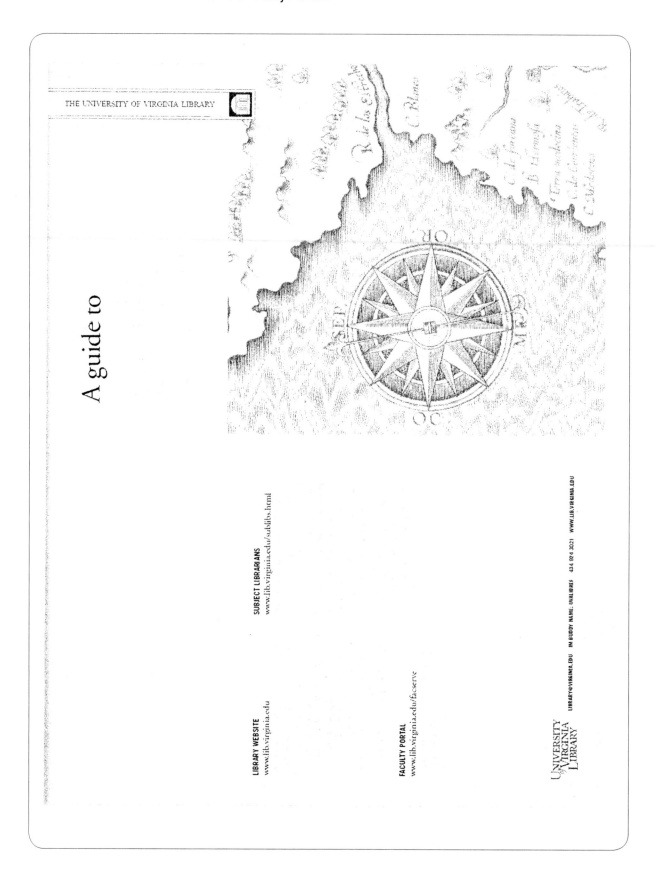

Faculty Services

LEO AND INTERLIBRARY LOAN SERVICES
www.lib.virginia.edu/leo

LEO (Library Express On-Grounds) retrieves books or photocopies from a U.Va. Library, remote holdings, or via Interlibrary Loans and delivers them to departmental offices. To request an item or set up an account, please visit www.lib.virginia.edu/leo. The account allows you to request and track all of your LEO, ILL, and Toolkit materials. Articles and papers will be scanned and delivered in .pdf format unless print is the selected preference when an account is set up. Material requested within the U.Va. collection will be delivered within 2-3 business days. Material obtained through another university will be delivered within 3-10 business days. For more information, contact leo@virginia.edu or call (434) 924-3875.

UVACOLLAB TOOLKIT
toolkit.itc.virginia.edu

UVACollab is the new ITC-supported course management software in use at U.Va., replacing Instructional Toolkit. UVACollab allows you to post articles for your classes to read, administer tests, conduct online discussions, and much more.

INSTRUCTIONAL SCANNING SERVICES
www.lib.virginia.edu/scan/index.html

Instructional Scanning Services (ISS) is part of a suite of services to support the U.Va. faculty in your use of electronic materials for instruction. ISS will scan materials into a PDF format and upload them to your UVACollab site, link materials already in electronic format to the Instructor's course site, and scan materials for other instructional uses.

Computers

RESERVES

Faculty can have their own or Library books and other physical materials such as videos and CDs reserved at many of the libraries for use by students in their courses.

PURCHASE REQUESTS

Items that you would like to be added to the Library collection can be requested at the URL above.

LIBRARY INSTRUCTION

Librarians are available to conduct class instruction sessions in your classroom or in the Library. To request a session, just contact your subject librarian using the URL above.

NOTICES

The Library sends recall, hold, overdue, and billing notices by e-mail.

CIRCULATION

As faculty, you may check out books from all libraries indefinitely; however, all are subject to recall by other users. If renewal is necessary, most materials may be renewed via VIRGO, telephone, or in person. Books may be returned to any library location or in the bookdrop behind Alderman Library. Reserve material should be returned to the library from which they were borrowed.

RESEARCH ASSISTANT PRIVILEGES

Borrowing privileges may be requested for research assistants of faculty members. An application is available at the Alderman Library circulation desk.

UNIVERSITY LIBRARIES COMMITTEE

The Libraries Committee is appointed annually by the president of the University. The Committee considers and reports to the president on the larger questions of library service to the University community and on long-range library planning. More information can be found at

THE SCHOLARS' LAB

The Scholars' Lab is a high-tech facility for study and research located on the main floor of Alderman Library. Combining the services of the Library's GeoStat and E-Text centers and ITC Research Computing Support, the Scholars' Lab offers four thousand square feet of space for work on collaborative projects, and access to Library staff expertise in electronic encoding and digitization, programming and information design, geospatial and statistical data analysis, and the use of U.Va.-licensed software.

RESEARCH COMPUTING LAB

The Research Computing Lab in the Brown Science and Engineering Library offers technical support for high performance and scientific computing. Advanced consultation services in areas range from data management and metadata to computational science and visualization. Students, faculty, and researchers from all disciplines are welcome.

DIGITAL MEDIA LAB

The Digital Media Lab, located on the third floor of Clemons Library, serves students, faculty, and staff. Comprised of reserve-able Macintosh workstations with entry-level and sophisticated production software, the lab has consultants and staff that provide one-on-one instruction. Walk-ins are also welcome. Focusing on the convergence of media and technology, the Lab assists digital imaging, audiovisual production, post-production, physical interactivity, 2D/3D animation, mobile technologies, as well as visualization and delivery of media content. The DML circulates a small collection of entry-level and sophisticated production equipment to support curricular activities.

DIGITIZATION AND PUBLISHING SERVICES

Digitization and Publishing Services, located in the Albert and Shirley Small Special Collections Library, provides digitization services of primary and secondary materials from the University of Virginia Library's special collections.

Front Cover Image

Detail from Cornelius Wytfliet's atlas *Descriptionis Ptolemaicae augmentum sive Occidentis notitia ....* (Louvaine, 1597) from the exhibition "On the Map: The Seymour I. Schwartz Collection of North American Maps, 1500-1800." Exhibits and other collections in the Harrison Institute/Small Special Collections Library are open to faculty teaching use.

Spine Image

A shelf of books in Alderman Library.

Image from Johanna Drucker's *Nova Reperta*, part of the faculty project Artists' Books Online (www.artistsbooksonline.org), created in collaboration with the Scholars' Lab.

A letter from Thomas Jefferson to Peter S. Duponceau, December 1820, part of the Albert H. Small Declaration of Independence Collection.

Associate professor David Germano and Director of Digital Research and Scholarship Bethany Nowviskie work on the Tibetan and Himalayan Digital Archive in the Scholars' Lab.

The largest of its kind in a research library, the new "Cruse" scanner in the Albert and Shirley Small Special Collections Library captures maps as large as four by eight feet and even scans 3-D items.

Cover of "Chariot Race" (1894) by E.T. Paull, one of the 2,201 copies of digitized sheet music to be available online fall 2008 for faculty and student use.

Cushing/Whitney Medical Library

Library Liaisons by Department
www.med.yale.edu/library

Yale Department/Program	Library Liaison
Allergy and Clinical Immunology	Mark.Gentry@yale.edu
Alumni Affairs	Toby.Appel@yale.edu
Anesthesiology	Denise.Hersey@yale.edu
Boyer Center for Molecular Medicine	Judy.Spak@yale.edu
Cancer Center	Denise.Hersey@yale.edu
Cardiovascular Medicine	Mark.Gentry@yale.edu
Cell Biology	Judy.Spak@yale.edu
Cellular and Molecular Physiology	Judy.Spak@yale.edu
Center for Interdisciplinary Research on AIDS (CIRA)	Matthew.Wilcox@yale.edu
Center for Medical Informatics	Hongbin.Liu@yale.edu
Child Study Center	Jan.Glover@yale.edu
Clinical Scholars Program	Jan.Glover@yale.edu
Combined Program in the Biological and Biomedical Sciences (BBS)	Judy.Spak@yale.edu
Comparative Medicine	Matthew.Wilcox@yale.edu
Deans and Administrations, YSM	Charles.Greenberg@yale.edu
Dentistry	Jan.Glover@yale.edu
Dermatology	Lynn.Sette@yale.edu
Diagnostic Radiology	Holly.Nardini@yale.edu
Digestive Diseases	Mark.Gentry@yale.edu
Endocrinology and Metabolism	Mark.Gentry@yale.edu
Epidemiology and Public Health	Matthew.Wilcox@yale.edu
Genetics	Judy.Spak@yale.edu
Geriatrics	Mark.Gentry@yale.edu
Hematology	Mark.Gentry@yale.edu
History of Medicine	Toby.Appel@yale.edu
Human Investigation Committee	Charles.Greenberg@yale.edu
Humanities in Medicine	Toby.Appel@yale.edu
Immunobiology	Judy.Spak@yale.edu
Infectious Diseases	Mark.Gentry@yale.edu
Institutional Animal Care and Use Committee	Matthew.Wilcox@yale.edu
Internal Medicine, General	Mark.Gentry@yale.edu
Laboratory Medicine	Judy.Spak@yale.edu
Microbial Pathogenesis	Judy.Spak@yale.edu
Molecular Biophysics and Biochemistry	Judy.Spak@yale.edu
Nephrology	Mark.Gentry@yale.edu
Neurobiology	Lei.Wang@yale.edu
Neurology	Lei.Wang@yale.edu
Neurosurgery	Lei.Wang@yale.edu
Nursing, School of	Janene.Batten@yale.edu
Obstetrics, Gynecology and Reproductive Sciences	Holly.Nardini@yale.edu
Ophthamology and Visual Science	Cynthia.Crooker@yale.edu
Orthopedics and Rehabilitation	John.Gallagher@yale.edu
Pathology	Judy.Spak@yale.edu
Pediatrics	Lynn.Sette@yale.edu
Pharmacology	Judy.Spak@yale.edu
Physician Associate Program	Jan.Glover@yale.edu
Postgraduate and Continuing Medical Education	Mark.Gentry@yale.edu
Psychiatry	Jan.Glover@yale.edu
Public Health, School of	Matthew.Wilcox@yale.edu
Pulmonary and Critical Care Medicine	Mark.Gentry@yale.edu
Rheumatology	Mark.Gentry@yale.edu
Surgery	Charles.Greenberg@yale.edu
Therapeutic Radiology	Judy.Spak@yale.edu
Women in Medicine	Toby.Appel@yale.edu
Yale-New Haven Hospital	Mark.Gentry@yale.edu

Liaisons—
Your link to the library

Consult · Inform · Support

We would be happy to arrange one-on-one consultations with any faculty member, resident, postdoc, or staff member. For example, we can help you:

WORK MORE EFFICIENTLY
- Advanced techniques to search biomedical literature
- Save a search strategy and receive email updates
- Receive the Table of Contents of a selected journal via email
- Search resources for cited references
- Learn RefWorks or EndNote to organize articles and format manuscripts
- Use Quosa to manage your PDFs
- Use YaleLinks to link to the full online article
- Access journal articles from off campus

LEARN NEW SKILLS
- Services to help with specific tasks
- Resources for PDAs and other handheld devices
- Information and assistance as you publish
- Resources for evidence-based clinical practice
- How to use new resources — Scopus and Quosa

SUPPORT DEPARTMENTAL TEACHING AND PUBLISHING
- Information on NIH Public Access Policy
- Highlight appropriate library resources for grant applications

Partnership Agreement

Agreement Between
University of Washington Libraries
and
UW Office of Learning Technologies

This agreement is between the UW Office of Learning Technologies (OLT) and UW Libraries for provision, management and client support of computing technologies available across multiple library units. This includes:

- 279 authenticated public workstations located in the following libraries: Architecture and Urban Planning, Drama, East Asia, Engineering, Foster, Fisheries-Oceanography, Odegaard Undergraduate, Social Work, and Suzzallo and Allen. OLT charges a fee to UW Libraries for support of these workstations. Budget and payment details are included in Attachment 1.

- Two computerized training facilities in the Odegaard Undergraduate Library (OUGL). They are located on the first floor of OUGL in rooms 142 (Collaboratory I) and 102 (Collaboratory II).

- Five technology studios, located in Suzzallo Library 1st floor corridor (Collaboration Studio 1), OUGL 2nd floor (Collaboration Studios 2 and 3), OUGL 216 (Digital Audio Workstation Studio), and OUGL 334 (Digital Presentation Studio).

- One videoconference facility located in OUGL 320.

- One learning commons with approximately 365 workstations, located on the second floor of OUGL.

Statement of Use

The Office of Learning Technologies, in collaboration with the UW Libraries, will provide and manage 279 UWNetID-authenticated general-access workstations located in ten University Libraries facilities; maintain the two Odegaard collaboratories; five technology studios, one videoconference studio, and the large general-access learning commons in OUGL.

UW Libraries will provide space, furniture, building security, and library staff in support of these facilities. OLT will seek funding from the Student Tech Fee Committee and other appropriate funding sources for hardware and software purchases. OLT will provide staff to install and maintain computing equipment, and appropriate programs and services to support client use of these learning technologies and associated spaces.

Equipment Installation and Licensing

1. OLT will provide hardware, current operating system software, and current desktop application software for all workstations. In instances where special software is required (some specialized libraries), the purchase of said software will be negotiated between both parties. OLT will make every effort to secure software funding from outside sources (STFC, etc.), but in some cases the specific library or associated academic department may need to make the purchase.

2. The Libraries will provide space (and some furniture) in which the workstations will be installed and configured for client use and sufficient power and networking infrastructure to support normal usage of the workstations. Replacement of current furniture will be a joint responsibility to purchase or seek external funding.

3. Hardware and software will be imaged, tested, and available for use by the beginning of each quarter. Security patches, etc will be added throughout the quarter as they become available.

4. The overhead projectors and screens in the Collaboratories were acquired through joint purchase of UW Libraries and OLT and will remain in the OUGL collaboratories until they can be replaced. (Funding has been provided by ATAC to replace the projectors in the 06/07 academic year. OLT will provide funding to cover installation and new mounting/security cages.)

5. All hardware and software covered under this agreement will be purchased, installed, maintained, and inventoried by OLT. The equipment will remain in the named University Libraries facilities until upgraded or until the termination of this agreement, whichever comes first. Replaced and/or upgraded machines will be repurposed or sent to surplus by OLT.

Maintenance, Support, and Software Installation and Upgrades

6. Maintenance of the workstations by OLT will include:
    a. Ensuring the proper functioning of the network and all peripherals.
    b. Ensuring that software specified in this agreement and approved in the future is installed and running correctly.
    c. Maintenance of all workstations, so that, in any location, 90% of the machines will be functional. Exceptions will include planned outages for maintenance, which will typically occur during quarter breaks and equipment failure beyond our control.
    d. Ensuring that the Associate Dean of Libraries for Research and Instructional Services and the Director of OUGL or their designees are notified immediately of any broad equipment or software failures that impact service such that less than 90% of the workstations are out of service. They will not be notified of machine problems that occur within or less than the 10% margin, or of outages outside the control and responsibility of OLT (such as network outages). Both parties will be notified in advance of any planned outages, such as maintenance during quarter breaks.
    e. Infrastructure and machine support via phone as well as in person, as warranted, between 8:00 A.M. and 5:00 P.M Monday-Friday.
    f. Monitoring of machines for service levels and security will be accomplished by physical monitoring by the OLT team on a routine schedule, including regular walkthroughs of all spaces and by electronic monitoring through the OLT LabTracker software (or some equivalent). All problems recorded and tracked with the OLT LabTracker software (or some equivalent).
    g. Image configuration frozen at the beginning of every quarter to ensure stability and consistency.
    h. Support during all scheduled activities in the Odegaard collaboratories and Videoconference Studio. Support will be available via phone as well as in person, between 8:00 A.M. and 5:00 P.M, or by pre-arranged appointment.

7. All requests to install or remove software from the image must go through OLT for approval. Any additional software installation requests must be accompanied by software licenses and must be compatible and consistent with the OLT image paradigm. Any changes that substantially impact the user experience or the capabilities of the workstations must also be approved by the Libraries (e.g., changing O/S versions, application software versions, etc.). OLT staff will approve and install

software. Should disagreements about the software image and workstation configuration arise, OLT and the Libraries will discuss the situation and arrive at a mutually agreeable solution.

8. Standard OS and applications software upgrades will be conducted during quarter breaks in conjunction with lab upgrades. OLT makes every effort to have workstations running the most current software; however, on occasion upgrades may not be done if OLT determines such upgrades could adversely affect the workstations.

9. All software installed on the workstations must be legally licensed. OLT will maintain software licenses for all software purchased and installed by OLT. Clients must provide OLT with licenses for all requested software installations.

Policies

10. Neither OLT nor the Libraries will be solely responsible for hardware or software costs outside those provided for by the STF grant. If extraordinary, unanticipated expenses arise; the parties will discuss the situation and arrive at a mutually agreeable solution.

11. Individual faculty, instructors, or students may not install software on any of the machines in the Odegaard Collaboratories or reconfigure any of the equipment. All changes must be requested through OLT. Instructor's software approved for installation by OLT will be the responsibility of each instructor. OLT will not support software use beyond installation.

12. All users of the workstations agree to abide by the OLT and Libraries usage policies. OLT and the Libraries will make written copies of these policies available to each other.

13. OLT and the UW Libraries reserve the right to prohibit use of a workstation by any individual who violates the usage policies, in accordance with the Policy on Libraries Disruptions (Libraries' Operations Manual, Vol. 1, Section B, No. 4), the University Libraries Code of Conduct (Libraries' Operations Manual, Vol. 1, Section B, No 4, Appendix A.) and the UW Libraries Computer Use Policy

Scheduling, Access, and Room Use

14. The OLT Ed-Tech Manager is responsible for scheduling the OUGL collaboratories and the Video Conference Studio.

   UW Libraries receives priority use of Collaboratory II, Mon-Fri., 9:30 a.m.-2:30 p.m. This time will be blocked out exclusively for UW Libraries use until two weeks prior to the booking event.. Within two weeks of booking date, if the space is not reserved by the UW Libraries, the OLT Ed-Tech Manager may make the room available for other use....
   The OVCS partners (UW Libraries, OLT, and C&C) will receive priority and free use of the Videoconference Studio. Specific logistics are outlined in the OVCS partners MOU.

15. Clients may reserve the Technology Studios via the UW Libraries booking system. Clients may reserve the Videoconference Studio, Collaboratory 1, and Collaboratory 2 via the Catalyst website reservation form. Requests will be processed and responded to within 48 hours.

16. The Collaboratories and Video Conference Studio will are not available for unscheduled or unattended client access. This clause does not apply to the UW Libraries.

17. Consulting and staffing by the OLT Ed-Tech Manager will include a brief (10 – 15 minute) orientation for each instructor scheduled to teach in a collaboratory, arranged in advance of the first day of class. The orientation will include the equipment, services provided, and usage policies.

18. Consulting and staffing by the OLT Videoconference Consultant will include an orientation for each primary client scheduling a video conference, arranged in advance of the videoconference. The orientation will include the equipment, services provided, and usage policies. The VCC will also coordinate and test with the distant end prior to the scheduled videoconference.

19. OLT will provide consulting regarding the hardware, software, and services in the facilities, at no cost to UW Libraries. The UW Libraries will not be charged for use of the facilities. If extraordinary, unanticipated expenses arise, the parties will discuss the situation and arrive at a mutually agreeable solution.

20. All users of the collaboratories (students and instructors) agree to abide by the OLT usage policies. OLT will make written copies of these policies available to UW Libraries staff. The OLT Ed-Tech Manager will also forward a copy of these policies to every instructor scheduled to teach.

21. All persons, including maintenance personnel, will gain access to the Odegaard Collaboratories, Videoconference Studio, and Technology Studios via the Information/Circulation desk. Each time they are finished using the room, instructors will be responsible for securing the Odegaard Collaboratories and returning the keys to the Information Desk

Terms of Agreement

22. This agreement will be in effect for three years, beginning July 1, 2006. The conditions of the agreement will be reviewed annually, prior to, or no later than June 30, 2007, 2008 and 2009 by all parties for additions or revisions.

23. If either party wishes to terminate this agreement prior to the end of the three-year period, termination conditions will be mutually agreed upon, with at least three months notification required.

[Name], Vice Provost, Educational Partnerships and Learning Technologies   Date

[Name], Dean, University Libraries   Date

SELECTED RESOURCES

DOCUMENTS

Beagle, Don. "Extending the Information Commons: From Instructional Testbed to Internet2." *Journal of Academic Librarianship* 28, no. 5 (2002): 287–96.

Bennett, Scott. *Libraries Designed for Learning*. Washington, DC: Council on Library and Information Resources, 2003. http://www.clir.org/pubs/reports/pub122/pub122web.pdf

Brewer, Joseph M., et al. "Libraries Dealing with the Future Now." *ARL: A Bimonthly Report on Research Library Issues and Actions from ARL, CNI, and SPARC* no. 234 (June 2004): 1–9. http://www.arl.org/bm~doc/dealing.pdf

Campbell, Jerry D. "Changing a Cultural Icon: The Academic Library as a Virtual Destination," *EDUCAUSE Review* 41 (Jan./Feb. 2006): 16–30. http://connect.educause.edu/apps/er/erm06/erm061.asp

Chrzastowski, Tina E., and Lura Joseph. "Surveying Graduate and Professional Students' Perspectives on Library Services, Facilities and Collection at the University of Illinois at Urbana-Champaign: Does Subject Discipline Continue to Influence Library Use?" *Issues in Science & Technology Librarianship* no. 45 (Winter 2006) http://www.istl.org/06-winter/refereed3.html

Crockett, Charlotte, Sarah McDaniel, and Melanie Remy. "Integrating Services in the Information Commons: Toward a Holistic Library and Computing Environment." *Library Administration and Management* 16, no. 4 (2002): 181–86.

Engel, Debra, and Karen Antell. "The Life of the Mind: A Study of Faculty Spaces in Academic Libraries." *College and Research Libraries* 65, no. 1 (January 2004): 8–26. http://www.ala.org/ala/mgrps/divs/acrl/publications/crljournal/2004/backjan2004/engel.pdf

Goldenberg-Hart, Diane. "Enhancing Graduate Education: A Fresh Look at Library Engagement." *ARL: A Bimonthly Report on Research Library Issues and Actions from ARL, CNI, and SPARC* no. 256 (February 2008): 1–8. http://www.arl.org/resources/pubs/br/br256.shtml

Haas, Leslie, and Jan Robertson. *The Information Commons*. SPEC Kit 281. Washington, DC: Association of Research Libraries, July 2004. http://www.arl.org/bm~doc/spec281web.pdf

Hiller, Steve. "How Different are They? A Comparison by Academic Area of Library Use, Priorities and Information." *Issues in Science and Technology Librarianship* no. 33 (Winter 2002). http://www.istl. org/02-winter/article1.html

Lippincott, Joan K. "Linking the Information Commons to Learning," in *Learning Spaces: An EDUCAUSE e-Book*, ed. Diane G. Oblinger. Washington, DC: EDUCAUSE, 2006. http://www.educause.edu/ LearningSpaces/10569

Lougee, Wendy Pradt. "Diffuse Libraries: Emergent Roles for the Research Library in the Digital Age." Washington, DC: Council on Library and Information Resources, August 2002. http://www.clir. org/pubs/reports/pub108/contents.html

MacWhinnie, Laurie A. "The Information Commons: The Academic Library of the Future." *portal: Libraries and the Academy* 3, no. 2 (2003): 241–57.

Maes, William R. "Embedding Research and Learning in Libraries." *IATUL Annual Conference Proceedings* 16 (2006): 41–50. http://www.iatul.org/doclibrary/public/Conf_Proceedings/2006/Maespaper.pdf

Meyer, Richard, and Crit Stuart. "Evaluating Physical and Virtual Space to Support Teaching and Learning." *150th ARL Membership Meeting Proceedings*. May 2007. http://www.arl.org/resources/ pubs/mmproceedings/meyer-stuart.shtml

O'Brien, Linda, and Peter Sidorko. "Integrating Information, Education and Technology Services." *EDUCAUSE 2000: Thinking IT Through. Proceedings and Post-Conference Materials*. Nashville, TN, October 10–13, 2000. http://www.educause.edu/LibraryDetailPage/666?ID=EDU0027

Shill, Harold B., and Shawn Tonner. "Creating a Better Place: Physical Improvements in Academic Libraries, 1995–2002." *College & Research Libraries* 64 (Nov. 2003): 431–66 http://www.ala.org/ala/mgrps/divs/ acrl/publications/crljournal/2003/nov03/shill.pdf

Spencer, Mary Ellen. "The State of the Art: NCSU Libraries Learning Commons," *Reference Services Review* 35, no. 2 (2007): 310–21.

Note: All URLs accessed November 17, 2008.

S P E C K I T T I T L E L I S T

SPEC Kit Price Information

Individual Kits: $35 ARL members/$45 nonmembers, plus shipping and handling.

Individual issues of the Transforming Libraries (TL) subseries: $28, plus shipping and handling.

Shipping & Handling

U.S.: UPS Ground delivery, $10 per publication. Canada: UPS Ground delivery, $15 per publication

International and rush orders: Call or e-mail for quote.

Payment Information

Make check or money order payable in U.S. funds to the Association of Research Libraries, Federal ID #52-0784198-N. MasterCard and Visa accepted.

Send orders to: ARL Publications Distribution Center, P.O. Box 531, Annapolis Junction, MD 20701-0531
phone (301) 362-8196; fax (301) 206-9789; e-mail pubs@arl.org

Order online at: http://www.arl.org/resources/pubs/index.shtml